Sex Games for Couples

Naughty Games for Adults, Hot Quiz, Truth or Dare, Would you Rather and Sexy Toys Games for Couples

By

Rachel Bell & Tony Bravo

Table Of Contents

Introduction

Complicity is shared knowledge, which is unseen. A shared spirit simply "stands above" you. Complicity means you're logged in. A quick smile, expression, or gesture will deepen your complicity. You stand on common ground together. This is called complicity. How should I create it? By forming unseen ties with one another. Suppose you're out with your companion at a party. You can get a drink for yourself, and without even asking to get him what he likes. He might be talking with anyone. You're just passing by and giving him his drink because you know he wants it. Don't live around. Don't anticipate, thanks. Only give him a beer and carry on. For those who see it, this easy gesture means a lot. They see the connection as invisible. They view one another as having shared knowledge and deep concern. Do not use complicity as a way to monopolize your partner's attention. Give them space. The art of developing complicity is the art of introducing this form of subtle 'telepathic' invisible touch. Stay awake and conscious of the unseen connection. With some exercise, you can feel and know where he is, almost instantly. The intangible relation is complicity.

We have been married for over ten years now. Things were intense in the beginning as the excitement of a new relationship takes over every couple. But with time, just like many other couples, things started to fade as we no longer engaged in romantic aspects of a partnership. Every good thing requires constant energy, time, and commitment. But with a complicated life, we often forget the little things and take them for granted. Subconsciously, we lose the spark from our lives. That's exactly what happened to us. We felt okay with no time spent together or making efforts to ignite our sex life. The desires seemed to fade away, and the marriage looked like a dead end. But instead of giving up, we started exploring ways to reignite our sex life and make our marriage happy overall. Based on our experiences, we share certain little things and big ones as well that make a big difference in our lives and fuel the fire in our hearts.

Chapter 1: Couple Complicity

Complicity, as simple as it might be to say, needs two accomplices. In a couple's workshop, a guy was heard saying the following to a woman, "I can't have a connection with you on my own; you need to be complicit in having a relationship with me, or this won't work."

1.1 The Significance of Couple Complicity

Complicity means that all parties assume complete control of their separate commitments to the relationship, which renders them jointly accountable for the well-being of the marriage, recognizing that any decisions taken separately or collectively, for good or bad, have an effect on one another.

It involves standing alongside one another at great times and standing even nearer on rough moments – never being absent when needed, whatever the causes or circumstances – echoing the attitude, "Strong people rise up for themselves, but greater people stand up for their major others."

Complicity is the awareness that a situation arises when a man and a woman recognize that their different schemes can be best accomplished as a conspiracy.

Complicity often signifies that the parties concerned are dedicated to being entirely compliant in their obligations towards each other since one's loyalty to a partnership relies on one's dedication to oneself.

When you are not completely involved in your own life, you can't be fully active in a partnership.

The reward of complicity is not real unless it comes along with the reality of who you are. An ancient expression stipulates, "Justice not only needs to be served, but it also needs to be heard."

Similarly, with relationships, "Complicity should not only be done, but it must also be seen to be accomplished." It must also be done in such a way that it is an obvious effort that is built on trust and deliberate-reflecting the attitude "I am complicit with myself in complicity with you."

If we do understand the complexities of reciprocity, the idea of being involved in a partnership takes on additional complexity.

Reciprocating in a constructive way within the framework of a partnership means "giving your partner as much as your partner offers you in the spirit of prosperity," such that a structural discrepancy is not generated that one partner provides all and the other partner takes away.

Reciprocity occurs as both parties give and take in a manner that is consistent over time, and that leads to the wishes and preferences of all people, respectively.

Reciprocity is a corollary to cooperation, which helps to reinforce and strengthen the relationship.

Exercised over months and years, it adds to the cohesive mixture of personalities that make up the couple a rainbow of colors.

Never be taken for granted, the couples revel in each other's contributions as a testament to their rising affection.

Let's not remember that participation isn't a static thing; as the couples grow and alter, it develops and improves.

It is by yummy complicity that a couple can produce more of the stuff they want and less of the factors they don't want.

In a way, it's like they can tailor the partnership to become a representation of who they are and how they react to each other, collaborating together to put it to life. It relinquishes the notion of ever giving up on one another.

It is in the spirit of the wholeness produced in the relationship that the couples put into it, paradoxically composed of the individual components, that the threads of their desires weave the tapestry of their mutual life.

They should never underestimate the capacity of wonderful collaboration to embellish a friendship and enhance it.

"True love is a continually evolving feeling." The "self-expanding feeling" is driven by deception in the sense of long-term intimate partnerships, and it is the distinction that makes all the difference.

1.2 Common Couples Problems

Money

Enable me to put it straight: Money wars are never over money among couples. So if you want a currency dispute to be minimized, track it back to the uncertainty that drives it.

Instead of arguing for the sum of money wasted on who-knows-what, concentrate on what truly matters: (1) your fear of not having control on crucial things influencing your life, (2) your fear of not having stability in your future, (3) your fear of not having consideration for your beliefs, or (4) your fear of struggling to fulfil your goals.

Work

For you, I have two words: date night. I do know. You learned this a thousand times: do a night of a weekly date, or your family will fail. It sounds more like a threat than good guidance, isn't it? Yet it is a surefire means of mitigating workplace tension.

Despite this repeated advice, it does not seem like the message is getting through. How often married people, between the ages of 25 and 50 with two or more children, have a date night, here:

- Four percent once every week

- Monthly: 21 percent

- Once every 2-3 months: 21 percent

- 18 percent about once four to six months

- Once in seven weeks or less frequently: 36 percent

Yikes...! We can do better, and there is a good reason to do that. The University of Virginia's National Marriage Project recently released a report dubbed "The Date Night Chance." This research found that husbands and wives who set aside a dedicated time to mix and have fun at least one time in a week were about three and a half times more likely to report being "really satisfied" in their marriages.

Sex

I recommend focusing on solving "coordination failure" to keep sexual frustrations down and the marital bedsprings jumping. It is a common problem in marriages. The number one explanation couples mention not getting sex in their marriage is "So busy," quickly accompanied by "Not in the mood." Much of the time, its slang, intentionally or not, for getting sex drives that have not lined up.

So, start to talk about it. I can almost see you cringing when I compose this. For most people, it's as easy to think about sex as sleeping in a bed. Yet it's a dialog that is key to aligning the sex drives and eliminating disagreements. When the time is correct, once you're both relaxed and not blinded, ask each other to explain when you're most keen to go to bed. You may be surprised to hear your answers.

Children

The solution to almost any parenting conflict is to get on the same page and to create a coherent front. Otherwise, the kids are manipulating each other against you and adding heat to the parental flames. Conflict is diminishing as coordination grows. It might not be easy to agree with your spouse on the guidelines and norms you and your children are willing to enforce. That is why ironing out differences behind locked doors is the first order of business.

Don't try to resolve your parenting squabbles right now — while the children enjoy the show. The moment comes when the two of you are free to discuss your proposals and resolve trade-offs. Hold on together once you reach an agreement. When parents form a strong front, there's no room for I-told-you-so recrimination.

Chores

Let's face it — the bulk of housework wars happen when one partner holds track. That is a misconception. Marriage scales are always in motion, and only if you have a symbolic scoreboard built in your partnership, you are setting yourself up for trouble. Using the trade division method would do away with all that.

For example, Amanda is better and faster than Chris, both at making the dishes and at rearranging up around the house. She really does it in half the time it takes for him. Does it make sense for Chris to do either of those tasks, given this fact? Not quite. That makes sense is for Chris to refill their pet's water bowl and ready their kid's bedtime space. He organizes and monitors their budgets quicker too. He is doing it in half the time that Amanda would take. He's kind of good at ironing his own shirts as well.

You get the picture. It is pretty simple. Prevent trying to divide up the middle of the household tasks. Love is better lived when you don't try to balance out the scales.

Conflict is a fact of life but not a bad one. When you're your spouse hitting it up next — and you're going to — go ahead and fight it out, but battle it with the goal of getting closer, understanding him or her better, and loving each other well even in the middle of discord.

1.3 What is your Sex Personality?

That's answerable in a cursory way by what stirs you up. Consult the adult television, research the books, and see the responses. They are a good base from which to decipher your desires.

Nevertheless, you will need to do a little more than that to really understand your feelings about the topic. You'll need to go out to do something for it, encouraging yourself to try and see the stuff you're involved in. There is far more about recognizing yourself than just what turns you on and is not going to be obvious unless you have the knowledge of it.

Oddly enough, I just had a talk with someone who's just starting out on their trip on this. On this topic, he has plenty of expectations but no real experience. With people beginning that journey, I find that they often have certain misconceptions that may affect the ability to identify their own configuration and feelings that I usually try to help them fix. Typically, I hear any of the following subsets:

- "You can either be dominant or submissive" — no, most individuals are more inclined than their equivalents to a combination of one or the other. That's 99 percent one way for certain individuals, 1 percent the other direction, but don't pursue self-discovery without exploring options in your orientation or you're not going to discover anything.

- "You'll just know" — maybe, but most of the people I've spoken to still need the experience to find out the finer details and where they were willing to contradict their self-image (particularly with woman dominants or male submissive), it normally takes a little time to sort out the variance between what they felt they were meant to feel and what they actually felt.

- "There are only one true means of becoming aggressive or submissive" — no, there are very, very different styles of a role, role orientations, and play values. Look for the direction that seems good to you inside the strictures of consent.

- "It'll look like it's in the movies" — no and hell no. The media does a bad job of presenting partnerships in BDSM. Don't search for something that resembles a video you've watched or a novel you've read. Look for yourself to feel it when having to implement something dictated by individuals who have no understanding or knowledge about what BDSM is.

- "You've got to do things correctly otherwise you're not dominant/submissive" — BDSM is ... well, it's maybe better to speak about it as a skill otherwise art style. You learn you develop expertise, and you aim for some sort of collaborative performance. Whether or not your personality is superior or submissive does not cling on to excellence but on the trends that evolve with time through learn and ability learning.

- "You've got to be some kind of person,"-nope. There are elderly people, youth, skinny people, overweight people, fit men, couch potatoes, people of all ethnicity and economic backgrounds, and a country who practice or engage in the BDSM. The movies may treat BDSM like it has a face, but you don't have to own a leather outfit or be a model to officially 'be' in BDSM, in all seriousness.

I'd tell you not to be nervous, but I find a lot of people anxious about it. Instead, I would advise you to be open-minded and ready to explore the topic. That should tell you what you're into fairly quickly.

Chapter 2: Understanding Sexual Desires

Do you remember when you were first starting dating your wife? Remember the joy you felt, emotionally, and physically? So when you actually went to bed together ... oh, are you still blushed from experience? Were those your glory times of Sex — when romantic love was energetic, intense, and you couldn't wait to go to bed?

But now, after six years, maybe a child, and a mortgage, led to a change in things? You've probably changed. Your husband will indeed be happy to have Sex as much as he shaves, but it may have been one more item on the to-do list for you. If you are having Sex once a week, heck, you're happy, even once every two weeks.

2.1 Understanding Sexual Needs

You may be changing, and you and he may be having some differences. One way of bringing things into context is to talk of how you and your partner may differ in some ways. Every weekend, he likes to play golf; you'd rather curl up with a book. Every night, you might have ice cream; however, he is satisfied once in a month with it. Get the idea? As in many cases, when it comes to particular sex desires, you're special.

The problem is that there might be something more going on. After all, driving is only part of what makes desire. Another just-as-important part is motivation. Psychological and interpersonal factors that create a commitment or interest to be sexual with your partner are reflected in motivation.

For example, some studies suggest that if one partner in a marriage has a low sex drive, unconsciously "withholding" Sex could be a means of gaining control in the relationship. That is a reason, albeit one targeting Sex.

Or it may be a method to show your unhappiness regarding the partnership. In other words, if you're unhappy with your relationship, there's no interest in having Sex with someone you're not happy with outside the bedroom.

Still, in the partnership, let's say you are satisfied. Say you love your partner really, and you really want your sex drive to be as ... driven. Just now, you don't have the motivation to get it there.

Following are some methods that can help you rekindle your passion:

- Sit back, and speak freely and frankly about the sex drive discrepancies. Speaking about the problems will help enhance trust and contact.
- Tell your hubby/partner/lover that you can't reciprocate as often; however, you are flattered by an obvious sexual desire for you, and your love is strong.
- Clarify to the partner that telling "no tonight's not the night is not a personal denial. You claim no because of a sex appeal discrepancy — a discrepancy of desire.
- Work as a team to alleviate your defensiveness and settle your disagreements over how much you desire Sex.
- Aim for agreement. So, for starters, if your wife wants Sex five days a week, and you want Sex once a week (or less), maybe consider getting Sex for a while twice a week.
- Plan sex, much like you'd schedule a pedicure or haircut. You are, at the same time, placing yourself in a physical state of mind by bringing in Sex and spending the days prior to the "appointment," wondering about it.

Get another sit-down talk with your wife after a month. How are things going on? Does your partner feel more physically content? Do you feel connected? Would you two really like the lovemaking?

If so, it can be time to step it on to the next stage. Start by having another "sex date." Because that is the thing: the more frequently you make love, the more you might want to make love!

But, what if the reverse happens? Instead of needing to have Sex more frequently, you find your urge hasn't really shifted, and you just don't want to make love despite a couple of weeks' effort — not even twice a week. Now it's time to make sacrifices for your partner.

You'll be the initiator for next month, for example. You both agree that when you initiate it, you'll only have intercourse. See how that goes, and add up how often you've had Sex after a month. Ask how you all feel. If either of you felt that the amount of intimacy was troubling, that's when it's time for a professional consult.

Begin with your health care professional to make sure nothing else is medically wrong; then consider meeting with a sex therapist.

And notice, Sex itself is not the most essential element of any sexually-related issue, but how you talk about intercourse and your personal desires and satisfaction.

2.2 Quiz for Understanding Sexual Desires

1- How much would you have preferred to participate in physical contact with a partner in this last month (e.g., rubbing one another's genitals, offering or obtaining oral pleasure, intercourse, etc.)?

A. Not at all

B. once a month
C. Once every week
D. Once every two weeks

2- How often did you have sexual thoughts involving a partner over this last month?

A. Not at all
B. once a month
C. Once every week
D. Once every two weeks

3- How powerful is your urge to actually participate in physical intercourse with a partner while you have sexual thoughts?

A. Actually I'm not very interested in this
B. If my partner were here, I would probably go for it
C. I could take it or pass on it
D. I do wish my partner had been here and we could get going

4- How powerful is your ability to act on it when you see a human you consider sexually attractive?

A. I really don't feel any sexual desire
B. I will think about it on and off for a day or two
C. I might think about Sex fleetingly, but it quickly disappears
D. I will often fantasize about the person and sometimes masturbate thinking about them

5- How powerful is your sexual desire when you're in romantic situations (such as a candle-lit dinner, a walk on the beach, etc.)?

A. I like the romance, but I don't particularly want Sex
B. I get turned on and hope it will lead to a sexual encounter

6- How would you score your ability to act sexually with a mate, compared to other individuals of your age?

    A. Very low
    B. I think I am probably about the same as other people
    C. Maybe a bit lower than others
    D. I think I'm more interested in Sex

7- How often have you masturbated during the last two months (including touching your genitals for enjoyment, inserting something into your vagina, or trying to get an orgasm)?

    A. Not at all
    B. once a month
    C. Once every week
    D. Once every two weeks

8- How powerful is the urge to expose yourself to sexual behavior?

    A. I never think about masturbating or touching myself pleasurably
    B. I think about masturbating quite a lot

9- How long can you go easily without having any type of sexual activity, either on your own or with a partner?

    A. Probably a year
    B. Maybe a few months
    C. About a month
    D. No longer than two weeks

10- When I watch a sexy video or read a sexy novel, I...!

    A. Skip through the sex scenes--I think they are boring
    B. I have a fleeting sense of being turned on, but it doesn't last
    C. I find them fun to read, but they don't turn me on
    D. I get turned on, and I like to revisit those scenes to turn myself on more at other times

2.3 How should you Dress to Increase Excitement?

So my wife and I went and purchased new cotton panties, which I considered a little more attractive in which we could both be satisfied. It is important that what you buy and wear fits properly with you. And if you have body issues (most of us do!) seek to put them at the door while studying how to dress sexily. That's pretty obvious, but I have to say it to make sure I drive home the point: buy and wear clothes that highlight things you both love about your body, whether it's your breasts, your legs, or even your back; anything that makes you feel sexy. Your guy would love the commitment that you are giving to him, and his optimistic feelings would help you shine.

In the Bedroom

- **Casual**

Minimal makeup and clothing with small efforts, such as a pair of bootie shorts or one of his dress shirts. Throwing on a pair of heels transforms nearly any look you might use daily into a provocative "sexy feel." With his beloved shorts and bra, you can note that just strutting about nonchalantly, would transform his eye.

- **Lingerie**

Moderate makeup, in some way stylish hair (looking for a put-together look), and a wide range of lingerie; long and silky, or shiny and tight, or lacy and girly, etc. Putting on the final touches like shoes and stockings can enhance the feel.

- **Dress-up**

Suitable makeup for your theme (e.g., minimum and innocent for "school girl" versus "escort" dark and slutty), as well as properly styled hair.

School girls typically come with pig-tails! There are a number of common styles that you might dress up in, but here you also want to add a lot of diversity.

- **Props**

One way to enhance your "sexy feel" without trying to include a particular trend is by wearing one-piece fishnet outfits, a lot more erotic than lingerie. And shoes, of course!

Wearing nothing but a thong and those thigh-high boots is a look of its own way. While the height added by your heels can enhance those sex positions, be careful: I have almost gouged my husband with my favorite stilettos several times!

Outside the House

Discretion is crucial. Taking into account where you travel and what you are going to do. When you have dinner with his boss, an outfit that may be hot for a night out dancing together won't seem sexy. Yet there's always plenty of chances to wear & look good!

If you're wearing a nice dress or skirt for an evening out, amp up the heat by leaving your panties behind. This one is a bit of fun when you're at home, but a lot of fun when you're away from home. It fits especially well if the evening involves a chance for him to slip a hand up your leg (like the movies), and it doesn't work if you're somewhere it might make him feel uncomfortable (like dinner in the house of his parents!).

2.4 Most Common Error in Dressing for him and for her

Mistakes by Her

You have to feel comfortable at the end of the day. If you can't relax in your new corset or your new shoes are apt to sprain a foot, then your glamorous dress won't bring too much spice to your sex life.

Consider being as daring as you can. But if you don't feel very comfortable, here's a tip: Hold the lighting down the first time you wear a new sexy outfit for your guy. Just remember that pitch black isn't going to work, because if he can't see your dress and you can't see his reaction, you're sort of defeating the aim.

In addition to convenience, seek to bear in mind that your outfit is accessible. Unless you're experienced trying new outfits together, do your best to avoid anything that will take you more than five minutes to get out of to have great times together ... anything longer can actually kill the mood.

Don't spend too long getting ready ... My husband and I experimented with role-playing for the first time, it was important to me to get dressed up and feel as sexy as possible in order to really take on my part. After an hour of applying (and reapplying) makeup to pose like an escort and another half hour of selecting the right jacket, coat, coordinating nylons with no gaps and socks, I came out to see him almost asleep on the sofa.

Now anytime my wife needs to look and feel good, and she attempts to get ready in advance by making sure that she is freshly showered and washed and that her hair is curled. She likes to be really aware of how she is doing her makeup, enhancing features but not being handed over too heavily unless the situation demands it. Early on, she puts on her perfect outfit to make sure she won't struggle for a misplaced belt or string last minute, and love feeling sexy as well as imagining the smile on my face and the potential good times later on.

If you're satisfied and open to new ideas, he likes it when it comes to dressing up sexy for your man, then try to have a variety of sexy looks from informal and subtle to hot and racy. This way, you'll be able to maintain your guy's high level of sexual interest and desire for pretty much ever.

Keep in Mind

Men are very visual creatures, and if there's one thing that's sexier than you've dressed up in something hot for your partner, it's that layer of self-confidence you're going to wear when you feel sexy and want to display it.

Mistakes by Him

So awesome even I had one in 1991. I used to rock it out in my Fun Jeans / Cross Colors. This group is not restricted to shark tooth necklaces but includes all gadgets hanging from the neck that are innovative or influenced by nature. Keep it ultra-simple if you want to wear jewelry-either don't wear any or check out a guy called Johnny Ramli.

I shouldn't have to bang about this, but guys don't listen. You can never wear white socks with a suit or dark denim and boots unless you're in a hurry to reach a happy hour or stand in line for a spit roast. It is like driving while drunk; please don't. Get a cab, take black socks, and get serious.

No, no, no, and a little more no. I don't care what suit brand you're buying, or even if it's your dad's, you must always have a suit that's tailored to fit you. You need to appreciate the fit, no matter whether you're slim or a little portly. Keep in mind, you should feel like a King in a suit.

I can't say that in my life, I saw a lot of poor underwear, but I realize it's out there. If it's on the internet, then you buy it. It is also important to note that undergarments have a shelf-life. It's good to transfer them to the big underwear draw in the sky as soon as you see slight wear, smudges, or a funky odor. Underwear is cheap, so make a good investment.

2.5 Most Common Mistakes Regarding Sex

Mistakes Men Make

- **Sex begins inside the Bedroom**

Guys may turn on like a light, but arousal doesn't happen so quickly for women.

Pave the way by cuddling, kissing, and holding hands during the daytime. Have fun together, and show her that you appreciate her.

Feeling comfortable and confident in the partnership is crucial to really let a woman loose during intercourse. A deep hug can go further than you would have thought. "Hugging for 30 seconds activates oxytocin, the feminine hormone that produces [a] sense of attachment and trust."

- **Suppose you know what she Desires**

Today, as many women fake orgasms as they did 20 or 30 years ago. And if she doesn't enjoy herself, you probably won't know.

Don't worry about asking questions like "How does this feel?" Or "Do you like anything different? To put it another way, ask for instructions."

- **Stay with the Strategy**

Don't think "if it worked the first three times, it's going to work the next three times.

It can depend on her mood regarding what turns her on, and where she is in her monthly period. "Maybe her nipples are more sensitive, or her genitals are less tingly.

Pay heed to your companion. "Try various stuff to see how she's coping."

- **Keep it extremely Physical**

Expand the foreplay idea. Some people "concentrate on physical stimuli and mostly neglect mental stimulus.

While men get sparked by what they see, "females fantasize a lot as part of [the] arousal process during sex."

- **Expect her to have an orgasm during Intercourse**

Sex alone will not do the job for 80 percent of women. Why not? Most sex positions do not help activate the clitoris directly.

There are other ways to satisfy her. "Women climax from oral sex even more often than from intercourse. Also, consider Sex with the woman on top, or a vibrator designed to use by partners during sleep. "Men should feel relaxed, not intimidated, with sex toys.

To make her hit the sweet note when you have Sex, take time to allow her to get started before you move in. "The nearer women are as they initiate intercourse, the more likely they can get an orgasm.

- **Do not try Seduction**

Women enjoy being seduced. "Seduction is as important as, or at times more critical than, approach.

Whether it's oral, visual, or psychological, she says, it helps know what sort of turn-on your partner wants. "When you talk dirty over the mobile or the text, does your partner like it? Track your finger up the chest slowly? Flirt at a pub with her?

Also, if you like what you see, say so? "Let a woman know how desirable she is

- **Concentrate on ringing the Bell**

Most women tend to get an orgasm from the clitoral stimulation, but it is more complicated than you would expect.

Some men "don't recognize the clitoris anatomy. It's more than the tiny "button" you can see. Its nerve fibers spread across the vulva and inside the vagina. It's all potentially worth exploring for pleasure.

You should move back and forth. It will steal away certain women's enjoyment by paying such close attention to the glans at the top of the vulva. It's so delicate that too much pressure will hurt.

Mistakes Women Make

- **Not making an effort to Initiate Sex**

Most of us are worried regarding ladylike conduct. For fear of being considered rude, we don't want to look pushy or come on too hard. It is one of the greatest errors women make when they refuse to initiate intercourse.

Most guys feel like they're always the initiator, and this causes a difference in the partnership on the intensity scale, "he notes. Men generally want to be approached just as much by their partners as females do.

Holding onto old notions about sex roles also prevents satisfaction with our sexual relationships. They used to believe women are less interested in sexual activity, and I no longer want to say that. I think women are as interested in Sex [as men].

Show your interest from time to time by taking the first step. Your husband would definitely enjoy it, and you can feel a new degree of fulfillment in taking credit for your sexual relationship.

- **Worrying What You Look Like**

Starting to think about how you look during Sex will stop you from appreciating yourself, and will ruin your possibilities of orgasm.

"Don't think of the fat on your belly or makeup on your face." Focus on the joy of performing. You have to encourage yourself to have an orgasm.

"Males want their wives to give up in sex play, and that's not likely if she's anxious regarding her physical concerns.

 Men don't notice half the things females obsess about anyway.

"It's incredible what men don't notice when you're passionate, full of energy, engaged in them, and flexible."

There is an evolutionary explanation to our physical flaws for the selective blindness men show. People are searching (unknowingly, of course) of women who can carry nutritious children. Beginning millions of years ago, there lived on people who drew fertile women and had several babies — the ones who couldn't have died out. While maybe not as important today, the primitive process for survival lives on.

"Men are drawn even more to women who display signs of fitness and vitality and fertility. Instead of thinking about your waist and hip appearance, think about your level of energy, and your passion and confidence in it, "Fisher suggests.

- **Sex is a casual thing for Men**

We should all let go of old-fashioned ideologies, for example, that women are not intimate or that Sex is just Sex for men. "Sex is a really important activity for some men. Do not downplay it.

The research supports the idea that, in the sense of a committed relationship, both men and women find sexual intimacy more satisfying.

"Numerous statistical surveys make it quite evident that married partners are the people who have the highest content and the most active Sex. That says a lot about 'casual sex' failings.

The figures show that men are just as concerned about Sex and relationships as women. In fact, above 50 percent of women and 52 percent of men who entered a one-night stand revealed that they did so in the hope of creating a longer relationship. In fact, one-third of them did so. What can we learn?

"Never presume a man isn't romantic." Two major errors in this culture are that females are not sexual and that males are not as intimate [as women].

- **Thinking that he is always up for Sex**

Sure, most young teenagers are willing and ready whenever you ask, but not true of men. Everyday life's pressures — family, work, bills — may zap a man's libido. This comes to a lot of us as a huge shock, and sometimes his lack of involvement in Sex is something we take personally.

"It comes as such a surprise that [women] really don't accept it," Fisher says of the response that many women have when their husband suggests they're not in the mood for intercourse. "They realize that they don't often have an interest in Sex, but they always love the guy. But when they find out that he doesn't want Sex, they say, 'he doesn't want me.' Not true. He just doesn't want to have Sex.'

- **Not offering him Guidance**

We may feel uncomfortable communicating really openly about Sex, what we like and don't like, even with a person we've been with for a long period of time and otherwise feel close to. But this is the only way to accomplish pleasurable sexual intercourse.

"A woman has to bear responsibility for her sexual experience." No man can get a woman to orgasm unless she accepts responsibility for her sexual encounter. Even the best lover can't understand what she needs without letting him know.

The good news is men want to please women very much.

"When you can reassure them in a manner that doesn't harm their pride, they can understand. She recommends women to sandwich what they do not like between five things because he is listening. "You're not going to find out until you're in bed with him next time. But men are listening, especially if you are quite clear on that.

- **When he suggests something new, you get Upset**

It's normal to want to spice things up with a little variation after a pair have been together for a while. Only because your guy likes to try something new does not mean that he or she is unhappy with you or with your sex life. In short: Don't mind it.

Still, it's important to tune in your comfort zone.

"Nobody should ever feel obliged to do something in the intimate and personal area of sexuality they don't want to do." If your man wants you to do anything beyond your morals, make it known that it is off your boundaries and justify why. Do so in a caring way as best you may, of course. If it's something about you that isn't even a moral problem, but you somehow don't want to, then clarify that again. If it's simply a shocking request and you're uncomfortable about it at first, try not to react negatively. Let him know, instead, that you need some time to think about it.

Chapter 3: Sex Positions

Whether you are experienced or a starter, it doesn't matter, this chapter will give you a variety of new positions to try, and you may already be trying some of them, but it contains tips to make them even more fun. It contains positions both for beginners and experts. Feel free to try them the next time you jump into bed with your partner.

3.1 Sex Positions for Beginners

Face-To-Face

- **How to Do it**

Lie on your sides, and facing each other, push up on the bed slightly higher, so the hips are above your partner's. Wrap around them your top leg, and lead them inside. If it's an uncomfortable match, Lube will support it.

- **Why It's Perfect For Beginners**

If you're young, you'll be in touch with your partner to make sure that both of you feel comfortable. This is a comfortable place where you can rest — thoroughly invaded.

Missionary

- ### How to Do It

Make your companion shift
their hips higher up the bed while you tie your legs around
them if you initiate in a missionary. This will provide you a lot
of pleasure than the missionary.

- ### Why it's good for starters

Missionary is a perfect beginner go-to, but this variant is a
stronger orgasm stance. Plus, both of you are in a comfortable
position to just reflect on each other and ensuring that you
both get what you need.

On Top (Modified)

- ### How to Do It

Push your companion against the
wall or a sofa while straddling them
down. They can bend their knees for
even more closeness, so they're
helping to prop you up.

- **Why it's good for Starters**

This is a great position on top, but some women feel somewhat exposed or uneasy — especially when they're unfamiliar. This allows you to be in power but with an option that is more sexual and connected.

Doggy

- **How to Do It**

Rest on your knees and hands   and spread your legs to allow your partner to kneel behind you. Depending on your variability in height, you may need your legs further apart or nearer together.

- **Why it's great for Newbies**

Even though you're young, you may want to get more intensity. This position helps you to interact with deeper penetration and allows a clit play.

The Crab Walk

- **How to use it**

If you've ever taken a gym class as a child, then this position's name will certainly offer some insight into how you'll conclude this one. Practically, you and your partner are both trying to get into a pseudo-crab role. He was supposed to sit on the ground with his legs bent, his feet flat on the ground, and his hands in support behind him. You lower yourself onto his penis in the same position and face him, and start your bumping and grinding.

- **Why it appears to work**

This position is just wonderful for experts looking for things to spice up. The positioning helps you to monitor how deep it can get, and the angle provides room to introduce a vibrator to the mix as well.

The Bridge

We have a position again that reminds us of something important. Yoga, anyone? You want to lay on your back with this one while your partner gets to face you on his knees in between your thighs. From here, as you lift your hips up to touch his hips, you want to arch your back when he enters you. Depending on your height, you may discover that your feet won't be flat on the floor, but it's not like you put too much load on your back or toes as he supports your hips. When he holds firmly and thrusts in and out, your hips offer assistance to him.

- **Why It Works**

During this position, the angle at which his penis is in creates a very deep penetration, which stimulates your G-spot like whoa. It's always in this role that either with one of his hands, he can stimulate your clitoris, or you can do it yourself, either with hand or with a tool. Attaining an orgasm by actively stimulating both the G-spot and clit is virtually another world.

Sideways Straddle

- **How to use it**

It's pretty tricky to get into. It's probably recommended that you conduct a preliminary round with your clothing on, and you realize what you are walking into. But let me aim to make this one as easy as I can.

Initially, you want him to lay on his back, on the concrete, with both knees bent and both feet down. You're going to crawl on top of him at that moment, facing off, with one of his legs caressed between your legs while you're lowering yourself onto his penis. From here, you want to imagine that his body is a clock, and his head is at the twelve spots: "If you straddle his right leg, your body will point at about 7:30. You will be switched to 4:30 if you are on his left leg. From there, you'll essentially rock back and forth, rubbing against his upper thigh and pubic area. "It actually sounds tougher than it is, but it's at a level of expertise, so if you pull it off, you get to pat yourself on the back.

- **Why it appears to work**

This place is just about grinding and managing all the grinding, and you can determine whether and when you're going to peak.

The Cross

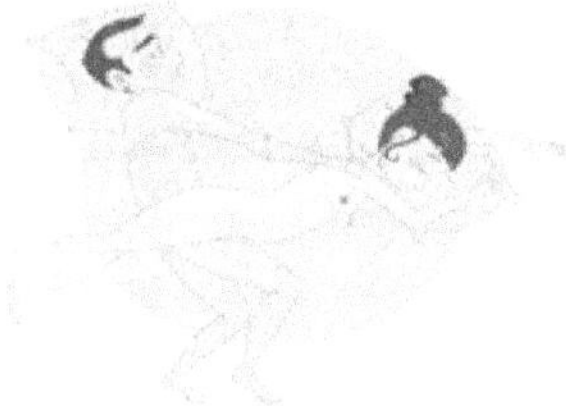

- **How to use it**

I adore this position, but to
be fair, getting around the first time is a little awkward. But it's just about taking things step by step, identical to the Sideways Straddle.

Let your guy lie on his side, facing you first. Next, you want to lie perpendicular to him on your back, because we are going to make a cross here as the title suggests. (And no, you don't have to be religious to do this.) From here, you want to take your legs over his hip as you push your vagina against his pelvic region and open your legs a little so that he can get in. It may look like you're sitting on his lap, but if that makes any sense, you're lying down.

- **Why it appears to work**

Besides getting you a gold star in the category of experts, this one works because his limited "range of motion" makes him last longer, and the angle provides great clitoral stimulation. It is perfect for those guys who are going too fast from zero to 60.

Chapter 4: Funny/Sexy games

4.1 Role-Play Games

Professor / Student

Who did not have the crush of a professor at one stage? Coping with the vision is important, right?

A trainer may be incredibly thrilling to know compassionately and lovingly (or sternly and dominatingly!).

Such scenes may contain 'reading' and assignments but also concentrate on old-fashioned activities, including spanking, paddling, caning, and other types of physical discipline, and on uninformed students who are arrested and imprisoned.

Find a fashionable school uniform for all sub-companies, and violate these rules!

Doctor / Patient

Clinical encounters between a doctor and a patient sometimes include a lot of uncertainty, anxiety, and concern that makes this style of play especially appealing to clinical enthusiasts.

Such scenes may include intrusive 'testing,' the playing of needles, enemas, etc.

Those in the BDSM society see medical fetishism as a particular form of an operation because special safety measures for the activities it includes are required. Make sure you have the critical details handled by a qualified expert.

I firmly recommend that you find a specific curriculum or laboratory in the near BDSM community that integrates these strategies, should you want to conduct a real-time analysis to integrate these items as scalpels, urethral activity or saline infusions.

Basic: don't do anything for which you are not eligible.

Caregiver / Little

It's a title often assigned to scenes of role-playing in which the top behaves like a father, mum, older adult, nanny, or a child nanny who performs the part of the person who is caring for. We've all heard the word "Daddy," adult kids, right? This is a definition of this nature.

This usually includes age, which indicates that the bottom deeds are junior or the top deeds are older.

It is a widespread misconception that age player is allowed by paedophilia or incest, but that is not the case. The draw here is the loving nature of the caregiver's role and mental independence to return to an infantile mind.

These scenes can involve children-oriented objects, including diapers, pacifiers, animals stuffed, bedtime, spanking, or other types of embarrassment combined with sexy action.

Kidnapper or Burglar / Victim

This can be an incredibly violent way to perform the role of aggression and consensus-based interpretation.

A mighty Dom acts as a kidnapper or thief, and his target is violently overcome.

Such a scene takes significant preparations for a safe and voluntary pull-out. Once you plunge in, you're going to want to do more work.

For some, abduction can become an unbelievably complicated multi-day dream, as abduction scenes are sometimes called. Several sex workers are often trained in fetish stimulation. It seems to be a fun holiday!

4.2 Soft Bondage Games

During Foreplay or Sex; Use a Blindfold on one Partner

It entirely puts the blindfolded partner at the mercy of seeing one, and the restraining sight makes all other senses erotically heightened. Here, a silk sash or men's tie will fit well.

The seeing partner runs a feather, long nails, fur, or nylon over their skin whilst the blindfolded partner lies down.

I advise beginners on this kind of sensory play. Take your time, and really play with your partner.

Increase intensity with Temperature Play

Run an ice block over their stomach, massage them with warm oil, or drip melted candle wax onto their stomach. (But not the "Anthro candle" on your nightstand! You can find a candle specially made for this play in your nearby sex store. They're typically called "massage candles" just FYI.)

Restrain the wrists of the submissive partner with a tie, allowing the partner to take full responsibility on top.

I suggest maintaining two fingers' worth of distance between the restriction and the skin to prevent injury to the nerves while securing the restraints. You may eventually graduate to four-point restraints (both ankles and wrists) and/or handcuffs for bondage.

Strip poker

Strip poker is an oldie but goodie, a surefire way to rekindle that passion.

Start with an equivalent amount of things for clothes, and subtract one object anytime you lose a hand.

If you're nude or nearly naked, switch on to pornographic acting if you lose a hand.

Sexy Ladders and Chutes

Buy a sexy board game, or make your own.

These games usually follow simple rules, but they require actions that range from the seductive to the truly wild.

Sexy card games operate along the same lines, involving partners to take turns in a variety of ways to please one another.

If you want to make your own, then follow the following steps:

- Write down sexual acts on each card, some mild and some exotic.
- Dump the cards into a cap or hat and take turns at random selecting a card.
- Whoever draws a card has to decide whether to act on the other individual or have the act done on him.

Truth or Dare

You need just you and your companion.

- **How to Play**

Take this as an opportunity to know more about your guy and pursue your craziest dreams of love. Take turns playing the fantastic game, making sure that your demands reveal what you really want.

- **Why**

Turns out Truth or Dare in middle school shouldn't have been left behind. Any pair can make it a very erotic game that will lead to lots of laughs, fun, and carefree foreplay.

- **Variety**

Take your stunts outside the bedroom and get all over your house for business.

Rolling the Dice

You Need: Two six-sided dies

- **How to Play**

Assign a certain sexual act to each value (and write it down, so you won't forget)! Perhaps one is he's rubbing his penis against your breasts, and another is he's going down on you. The game is not finished until all the 12 of you have gone around.

- **Why**

You're going to be encouraged to spend time on foreplay and have an increased sense of intensity about what's next? Surely by the end, you'll be triggered and ready for the big show.

Variety

One of you is even, and the other one is odd. Whatever you roll, this is the guy that has to be at the end of gratification that you serve. One more option? That individual gets to pick out what kind of foreplay you're making.

Strip Pong

You Need: 12 16-ounce single cups, Ping-Pong balls, a table for playing on, Alcohol of your choice

How to Play

Take it back to your college years and set up 6 Solo cups as if you were playing beer pong on each end of the table. Load the cups with your favorite form of alcohol — or water, if you choose to keep it safe — then stand with your friend at the other end at one end of the table. Take turns attempting to throw a ball of Ping-Pong in each other's cups. When one of you performs, the cup and a piece of clothing must be separated from the other. (Decide at the start whether the scorer gets to pick which item.) Whoever earns all six cups first gets to ask for the sexual favor.

Naughty "Would you Rather" Questions

- Hug and kiss next to a fireplace or light your fire in bed?

- Nude battle in a jello bowl or chocolate pudding?

- Make whoopee in a parent's bed or in a mattress shop?

- Send your boss a dirty text accidentally, or your mom a hot voicemail?

- Speak to me dirty over the phone or through text/photo messages?

- Have sex at the movies or in my car's back seat?

- Make love on the beach or in a whirlpool?

- Lose your sense of love during sex, or lose your sense of taste?

- Hot wax tease, or ice cubes?

- Role-play as a teacher's pet or play doctor?

Chapter 5: Tools for Helping the Couple

5.1 Beginners Kit

Handcuffs

Handcuffs are all about the mental and emotional turn-on instead of physical feel. "Discussing the scene you are going to set up and get the necessary consent can be very exciting." Because of the new media attention and normalization, it's awesome fantasy play and gaining popularity.

Just be careful — if you go for a super-authentic fantasy of prisoners involving real metal cuffs, they can hurt. "The soft, cushy ones are a must." I love to feel somewhat out of control when my partner handles me — especially when every other part of my life requires effort and care."

Clitoral Massagers

A vibrator that concentrates purely on stimulating the most vulnerable part of your vagina could be the perfect solution for women who have a hard time coming from other sex toys (or partners, even); I am a huge supporter of people who support their clits. "Surprisingly, men don't spend enough time playing the clitoris, and women keep quiet about their clitoral needs." While you're thrusting, use your clitoral massager; use it afterward when you're swollen, and he's fallen asleep; "let him see you using it, so it's becoming a couple of activities."

Nipple Clamps

Attaching these pieces to the nips hurts — but it's supposed to. So much of BDSM play is about the hurts-too-good kind of pain that can be a super-hot feeling for certain men if for no other excuse than the reason it's so distinct from what we experience on a regular basis.

Vibrating Panties

A very different type of hands-free vibrator, these pulsing panties make it as pleasurable to place on your underwear as it falls off.

Vibrating panties typically have to be within a certain span of turning them on from the remote or mobile. And for various conditions, there are a few common variants. Few high-tech panties deliver only a pocket for a rotating vibrator with bullets. You will move the vibrator directly to turn it on and off. Others have built-in vibrators that have a cord linking the remote to the panties. Wireless slippers are remotely controlled. Your partner will click on as a surprise during the day based on how far the remote may be from the slippers.

Rabbit Vibrators

What kind of rabbit should you ask? The bunny is better known to be displayed on Sex and Area, entering the vagina while fluttering on one's clitoris. This allows for the arousing of all areas at once. They typically contain or will propel, a range of speeds and settings.

Set the movements to your best moves and speed, then work your way up. Pulse the dildo end within, before you're at your most pleasurable, full pace. That can be hands-free if it thrusts.

Thrusting Dildos

By retracting and rotating back and forth, some of the newest and most creative sex toys to enter the market penetrate, thrusting dildos or "pulsators." They mimic penetrative sex, irrespective of whether you add them vaginally or anally.

Such evil guys take control of you, without raising a hair. A partner with thrusting dildos is typically not required, particularly if they come with a vibrator that stimulates your clitoris, rabbit-style.

Finger Vibrators

Generally, rubbery (or ridged) pads that you place on your fingers, these temptations transform your hands into vibrators, each finger being a dildo. They're normally made of an elastic ring with a pleasure-providing surface. The larger the projectile, the more powerful the emotions that it can offer.

Mount these shivering gadgets around your fingertips. They would also require lubricant — many finger vibrators are textured, so when used raw on a clitoris or other sensitive areas may sound rough. Trace the vibrators along with breasts, buttocks, inner thighs, and back to taunt the friend before moving it to more vulnerable places. Feel free to change where your finger perches — the lower down it lies, the further leverage you would have.

LELO Lyla 2

I think this is the best if you want a remote-controlled feel. You can wear it externally or internally (due to the tapered end it isn't ideal for anal insertion), and if you want to wear it out and about, it easily tucks into undies.

By simply shaking or tilting the remote, your husband (or you) can control the motion from up to 39 feet away. Very strong and very discreet.

Love honey Oh! Hot Knots Beginner's Bondage Game

For anyone who thinks of bondage, but is too confused to take the plunge. This fun tiny set turns your first erotic experience into a play, complete with a collection of 52 cards with instructions (like, "Blindfold your lover, then get them to please you using a method of your choice") - so you'll never run out of ideas.

Hitachi Magic Wand Rechargeable

For a function, the Hitachi Magic Wand is regarded as the "Chevy of Vibrators." It's big, it's strong, and it's reliable. Initially built to relax muscles, for its undoubted ability to relax people (particularly those with clits) in other ways, the wand quickly grabbed a cult following as a vibrator. While the sex toy works wonders to play solo, using it in a relationship to assist a partner with a vagina reach climax during sexual intercourse is fun. For those in BDSM, the masculine on the submissive partner frequently uses the magic wand to bring the sub to orgasm while bound or tied.

Cal Exotics Entice Tiered Intimate Rose Gold Nipple Clamps

Anyone with nipples will love clamping on nipples. Although the tool can be used alone, if you are pursuing BDSM playing with a partner can be particularly enjoyable. The dominant partner (the one who exerts control over the love scene) will typically put the clamps on the nipples of the submissive. This pair is good for beginners, as they are customizable. Start by placing the clamps with light pressure on the nipples, and adjust the tiny screw as wanted to tighten for more severe sensations.

B-Vibe Butt Plug Set For Beginners

Butt plugs are a must-have for any pair engaging in anal sex, so they do not need to be used solo: they may be used for dual-penetration with a partner during vaginal intercourse. Starting tiny is necessary, so this little guy is a great plug for beginners. Don't even neglect to use the lube as you put anal toys into your rear.

LELO Luna Beads Noir

To turn the heat on your foreplay sessions, this Keygel bead set is here.

Inspired by balls from Ben-WA, the Lelo Luna Beads is a set of two beads that are connected to a wire for retrieval. You may use them all at once or independently, but they promise to offer some intense, special pleasure either way. They can also be used anally or vaginally for creating a sensation for the upcoming night. The inner balls are intended to react with gentle vibrations to the action, making them suitable for use with a partner.

Liberator Heart Sex Position Wedge

Yes, well, it seems like physical-therapy support. But, for very good reason, the Liberator is a cult classic. It's an incredibly firm and reliable cushion that makes so many sex acts comfier (and very, very reachable, those hard-to-reach spots).

Use it during oral sex, under your pelvis. Try to use it for elbow support during ... anything that needs elbow support. For new or tricky positions, there really is nothing else like it. Sometimes, just a little boost is all you need.

Wicked Aqua Collection

Sex is great, but it's better to have sex with lube. There are plenty of lubricants to pick from. Choose the WICKED AQUA COLLECTION for a silky, luxurious experience that is Paraben-free. Flavors include Candy Apple, Mocha Java, Pomegranate, Salted Caramel, Vanilla Bean, etc.

Uber-Lube Luxury Lubricant

A lot of people get confused with lube, shouting insistently, "I don't need it!" as if the capacity to self-lubricate is assessing human worth. The fact is, even though you don't "need" lube, per se, it will make so many things more fun (and comfortable).

As the title suggests, Uber-Lube is the ultimate. Its silicone, which means it's hypoallergenic and won't be absorbed in your skin. The slipperiness lasts, the packaging is beautiful, and it stays on in the water, but with soap comes off easily. Plus, it's absolutely tasteless stuff. You're not "needing" oral sex lube, of course — but do yourself a favor and give it a shot.

Dame Products Alu

Calling all my ladies with susceptibility to hypersensitivity and/or yeast infection! Did I have a lube for you? Dame's latest Alu lube is water-based and pH-balanced because it won't irritate your vagina, and thanks to aloe, mushroom, and green tea extract, the material has plenty of cushion glides. If you are prone to chafing, this will prevent harm (and will not sting out any abrasions that exist). You don't even have to wait to put it on for sexy-time! Try a dab during the day if you feel dry or irritated.

K-Y Warming Jelly Personal Lubricant

Okay, so in the technical sense, this is not exactly an adult toy, but lube is a vital adult toy accessory. Lubricant is the WD-40 of sex, easing unwanted friction where lots of moving parts are present. K-Y Jelly is probably the most known lubricant on the market, and we particularly like K-Y Warming Jelly for its creative potential to cause a sense of warmth in addition to greasing those moving parts (and all your new toys).

5.2 Games with Sex Toys

ENDURANCE GAMES

While the gadget is on, you can't have any reaction. If you do, otherwise you have to pay a fine. Example: take a shot, reveal a secret, make a bet, and owe a favor, and so on. Locations may be everywhere - silent bar, band, club, mates' dinner, etc.

WALK THE LINE

See if you can walk a straight line while the partner controls the toy.

SPIN THE BOTTLE

Easy, but spinning a bottle, and whoever it falls on gets X-minute power over the product, seeing whether they can make the individual orgasm.

HAND OVER CONTROL

Strong, but fun. Offer the user the remote and let he/her lift or lower levels. Let the other person take a guess what level it's on. This is easier if you are able to agree on levels set in advance.

5.3 Dildo Play

What do you say, are dildos just for masturbation? You are incorrect, though. The dildos are often used during group play with the partner. Using a dildo while playing girlfriend will enhance your sex life together. If you've just used dildo for masturbation, then that is not your responsibility. Most people in India use only a dildo for masturbation. But let me make it explicit. A couple may use a dildo for personal gratification too.

I have been getting several questions regarding the dildo during partner play from the last few days. And if you do have some doubt regarding the dildo, then you can clear it up. It's really convenient if you choose to use your dream dildo for your partner — the only stuff you can do to accurately pick the right pair dildo with a dildo.

Now, you have a lot of doubts on your mind regarding the dildo couple or how the couple is using a dildo, which sort of dildo is better for the couple, etc. I realize you want to learn how to use a dildo in partner action too.

If you're a dildo lover and you just want a nice dildo in your personal life, then you can seek the dildo while playing partner. During partner sex, using a dildo is as easy as using it on its own during masturbation.

I say you can use the pair of dildo the same way you use a dildo in your masturbation period.

Choosing the dildo is the most significant aspect regarding the couple use dildo or pair dildo.

As you know, there are so many different kinds of dildo sex toys available in India and across the globe.

Yeah, determining which pair dildo is better for you if you haven't had a lot of practice with dildo sex toys or some other sex toys is a little complicated for you.

So here we're going to add some suggestions on dildo styles that will help you get more educated and help you pick the right dildo pair.

If you are a new person or you don't have a ton of knowledge regarding the couple dildo or dildo styles, then you can pick the tiny, slimmer dildo with a buddy for your first dildo use. There's even an alternative for novice users to choose the easy and compact dildo.

If you and your partner are still involved in using the dildo, then it is necessary to get the right model if you decide to engage yourself in anal dildo pair intercourse than you can pick the anal dildo.

Anal dildos are typically slender while dildo used to enter the vagina is accessible with loads of girths.

Now a day, some of the dildos are produced in such a way that they have a practical sensation. Generally, this form of a dildo is produced from the material that looks quite close to the truth. It is born of balls of nerves, scrotum, and testicles.

Both the couple can use that kind of dildo sex toy comfortably. Whether you are in anal play or practicing pussy doesn't matter when you would like to show the practical dildo, so don't hesitate to use the condom dildo.

Much of the practical dildo with the suction cup is usable, and it is simpler to use. This form of a dildo is often used for the couple who want to get interested in the pegging with a clip-on belt.

Any special form of dildo-sex toys included in this list. Specially built for the experienced consumer, this dildo sex toy.

If you have too many dildo sex toys encounters so consider this dildo. This form of a dildo is not used on the partner on both. This is designed particularly for women's and lesbian's simultaneous vagina and penetration.

As you learn, you can invest some time on foreplay or oral sex before you get interested in penetration.

If you're a dildo enthusiast, so you know how to use a dildo to improve anticipation and satisfaction in a particular way.

Yet if you are a pair of newcomers, then you can know about the usage of the dildo. It lets you having sex with your dildo.

If you like the external and internal stimulus during oral play, then dildo is the best choice for you. Also, don't hesitate to use dildo sex dolls with a personal lubricant or a lube. Attach the dildo gradually and gently after adding the lube and push it in and out or up and down according to your preference as well as your friend.

Communicate with your spouse while engaged in an oral activity, what feels good. Glass dildo and Metal dildo are the best oral play choice. This mixture of the dildo sex toys on your wife's clitoris, and your tongue and lips also bring her special satisfaction that she never felt before and is really explosive.

If you use a dildo instead of direct contact with a penis during sexual intercourse, then it allows the sexual behavior more enjoyable.

Using and put your own dildo into the anus, then push it up then down. You should always use the hand or arm to activate externally at the same time.

When you have a cock so you can quickly remove it at any moment with the dildo, it helps you to play dominant and submissive with simplicity and protection.

A dildo may also be used for the anal activity. Think thoroughly that you and your partner are up for it while using the dildo for anal sex.

The most significant aspects of anal play are that you can only use the anal lubricant. You should use your partner's anal dildo, or use your partner's anal dildo on you. It doesn't matter which person you are in a group.

If you don't want to mount the dildo when engaged in the anal play, so don't do it. Anal opening has a region abundant with nerves and use the dildo for stimulation and caressing. It's even bringing you the sensation of satisfaction.

You should always continue your anal play with a tiny dildo, and then step up to the bigger dildo once you get relaxed if you want the dildo products to be mounted than you want the flared based dildo.

Chapter 6: Role of Sex and Romance

It's an interesting moment to get married. If you want that your relationship becomes stronger for years to come, start by paying particular attention to your sex life.

As newlyweds, you probably don't think you need tips on how to handle hot and heavy stuff in your marriage. But aside from physical pleasure, there are many physical and emotional advantages to having a regular, pleasing intimacy with your partner.

Your sex life will profoundly affect the rest of your marriage. Emotional trust increases when you share intimate experiences with your mate. This can develop a solid bond of trust between you two, and can even reinforce monogamy.

6.1 Importance of Sexual Intimacy in Marriage

1. It Enhances Communication

One way you can strengthen Intimacy in marriage is by enhancing your communication skills.

You'll need to learn how to talk to your partner if you want a fulfilling sex life. Think about the bedroom appetites and dislikes. You can talk about what's comfortable with you, what's hurting and what fantasies are exciting to you.

Couples that know how to talk to each other have a considerable advantage over those that don't. Communication is how you get closer around each other, build confidence, identify issues, and resolve conflict.

2. It helps you to be Humorous

Let's face it: Sex isn't always the most deserving gesture. A loving act? Yeah. A graceful moving ballet? Difficult.

Sex can lead to moments of good humor. Your marital sex life will make you and your wife have a stronger sense of humor, from odd bodily sounds to hilariously inappropriate 'dirty talk.'

How important in a marriage is a good sense of humor? Very much! One research showed that people who share laughs together in their partnership felt more comfortable and fulfilled.

Further research shows that couples who are fond of laughing will have long term relationships than those who don't.

Also good for your health is a good sense of humor. In a survey of 20,934 adults, findings indicate that the risk of cardiac failure is lower among individuals who joke on a regular basis.

3. It helps boost Cardiovascular Function

The heart and blood flow are involved in the well-being. Studies suggest that sex may have a calming impact on the core that contributes to orgasms. It achieves so, partly, by producing the oxytocin hormone. This hormone has stress-relieving properties that reduce stress.

Another research indicates that people having sex at least twice a week are less prone to experience heart failure by 45 percent.

4. It helps improve the Immune Response

Yvonne K. Fulbright, Ph.D., and sexual health expert say couples who are sexually active take less sick days as compared to people who are not as busy in the bedroom. That could be because sex improves the immune response by growing the antibodies that battle germs.

Sex can boost your immune system with your metabolism, too. Studies indicate that mice who had an oxytocin deficit were more prone to become obese than mice who had stable oxytocin receptors. This research also indicates that oxytocin may have positive effects on metabolism.

5. Intimacy bolsters your Relationship

During physical contact, the oxytocin produced into the body may have a specific bonding impact on intimate partners.

Studies also indicate that the mechanism of brain reward which men experience during Intimacy can play a role in marriage male fidelity.

There is a close relationship between love and physical affection. Couples that love each other often tend to be more intimate in physical terms than those with rocky relations. Studies reveal that husbands and wives who were actively romantic together were among the best predictors of how often a person verbalizes their affection for each other.

Practicing everyday communication is the strongest practice you should take in regard to establishing a stronger, deeper bond with your partner.

6. Sexual Intimacy builds Trust in Marriage

When you and your partner have a regular, healthy sex life, you are continually improving your relationship of trust. This is attributed, in part, to the strong oxytocin produced during intercourse.

Oxytocin is a chemical that can influence human trust in the neuronal circuitry. In short, oxytocin promotes confidence.

This is largely responsible for bonding with romantic relationships as well as mothers and neonates. Oxytocin not only enhances trust in a marriage, but it also enhances emotional Intimacy, which could further enhance romantic relationships of trust.

7. It Fosters Teamwork

These three components are everything about marriage: partnership, coordination, and reconciliation. Your sex life is an interaction between two individuals, including all three of these qualities. You ought to love each other and appreciate each other. That needs both of you to interact with your spouse freely and display love.

8. It's all Enjoyable

Sex is supposed to be fun between married partners. It can certainly boost your health and happiness in your relationship, but it also feels good.

Orgasm activates endorphins that feel good and oxytocin that reduces the tension. Orgasm fills the body with sensations of joy, which are incredible. Who better than the person you love the most, to share this fun, interesting moment?

For a happy relationship, it is important to have fun recreational time together. One study reveals enhanced marital satisfaction when the couples find each other their best friend. It shows that people that take time to enjoy the company of each other, inside and outside the bedroom, will be happier in the long run than those who do not.

Sexual Intimacy is essential in marriage, no matter how long you have been married. Your sex life is improving your emotional connection and through your trust in one another. Regular, healthy sex life can also improve communication and has many benefits for health. Start off a healthy and happy marriage with a normal, fulfilling sex life.

6.2 Different Styles of Sex

What's a sexual style, then? It's about understanding how different elements of a couple's sexual experience shape a pattern — the way they initiate sex, how they embrace each other and participate in romantic scenarios, the role of coitus in their lovemaking, the interplay scenarios they choose, and the sense of sex for them and its place in their partnership. Sexual-style exploration concentrates on various main components. The first is how couples combine love and eroticism. Intimacy is about stability, predictability, closeness, and comfort, while eroticism is about taking emotional and sexual chances, adding excitement and imagination to sex, embracing unpredictability, and being able to let go and cherish sexuality for itself. Intimacy lets you feel safe in your sexual intercourse. It usually involves cuddly touch (handholding, touching, hugging) and seductive touch (cuddling, stroking, back-rubs, non-genital pleasure). Empathy towards the emotions of the friend, and exchanging sexual and non-sexual encounters, are the main values. Most people think Intimacy is crucial to a mature sexual relationship.

The second core element of sexual style concerns a balance between personal autonomy and emotional closeness. The obstacle is how each partner can preserve a sense of identity and at the same time experience a feeling of being part of an intimate, erotic team — how the "sexual voice" of each partner combines with the feelings and preferences of the other partner so that both partners can enjoy sex comfortably, pleasurably, and emotionally and sexually satisfyingly.

I found it helpful when dealing with couples who have entered a sexual impasse to explore the variety of sexual types from which married people cobble together their specific attitude to romantic and emotional connection — almost always without much debate or deliberate deliberation. To be sure, there is no one perfect sexual style for a couple; every style has its strengths and drawbacks. Furthermore, such types are not "pure" and do not reflect a comprehensive list of ways in which a pair may find sexual satisfaction, but provide an outline that offers a viewpoint on the preferences and choices of the couple.

The large majority of couples in my clinical experience usually fall within one of the four styles.

True love Couple Style

Soul mate couples love to share perceptions and emotions and give high priority to satisfying the needs of each other. They are lovers and best friends, who value the highest level of Intimacy with an emphasis on unconditionally loving each other and embracing each other just as they are.

When it works, this technique comes as close as any human relationship can meet virtually every need for closeness, security, and eroticism that a person has. The important word here is "when it works," as often it does not. Many people find that too much affection can undo sexual desire. Because eroticism requires a certain "edge," soul mate partners can de-eroticize each other by feeling so fully in emotional sync that it leaves no room for mystery or erotic playfulness.

Traditional Sexual Couple

These couples respect mutual commitment and safety above all else. Strong norms exist for conflict avoidance and strong emotions, especially anger. Both partners favor traditional roles to gender, avoiding drama. The man is the sexual initiator in those relationships; the woman is open to his proposals, imbuing the relationship with kindness and Emotional Intimacy. This is the least alluring type, with reduced priority being given to sex.

Seeing that the social expectations and guidelines are simple, in this style, sex never becomes a controversial topic. Traditional partners can embrace a more affectionate, though non-sexual, marriage than partners with other romantic types (though this flexibility may be a pitfall). In several partnerships, that style doesn't fit, particularly in partners that respect gender equality.

Emotionally Expressive romantic Couple

This is the "fun and erotic" erotic style full of strong feelings and drama that is frequently seen in films. Partners are free to share their enthusiasm, in word and deed, both positive and negative. The sense of vitality and adventure that imbues this style often leads to environmental stimulation such as porn videos and sex toys being used and/or sexual fantasies being played out. Partners are experiencing high spontaneity, vitality, and unpredictability. Yes, they fight, often with no holds barred, but after a conflict, they use intercourse to make up, and on the whole, their sexuality keeps them resilient. But this is the most volatile and unstable sexual style, which means emotional and sexual disputes can explode into fury and sudden, dramatic relationship dissolution.

Complementary sexual style among couples

Each participant feels free to initiate Intimacy in the complementary style (the most growing sexual style), to say no, and to suggest a particular sensual or romantic scenario. In fact, both partners recognize that sharing responsibility for the strength of the experience is the best aphrodisiac for both. Both realize it is not the role of the other person to give a desire or orgasm to their partner. They are instead receptive and responsive to the sexual feelings and preferences of one another.

Having "his," "her," and "our" bridges to sexual desire, these couples are really comfortable. But once a couple has established a sexually satisfying partnership, going on automatic pilot is always in danger. The ongoing sexual connection of a couple is a dynamic experience: it takes fresh inputs and new energy.

6.3 Why Romance is Important?

Romance is one of the most important features of relationship happiness. The value of passion cannot be trivialized in a friendship.

Still, many partners don't really understand how important a relationship is to passion or the advantages of romance.

Recognizing how important affection is in a marriage and why affection is important in a relationship is so essential to those interested in reigniting love and is a necessary first step.

So what are the tiny things you did as part of your wedding romance to get his affection, to keep him happy, to win over him? We'd be willing to bet these things don't happen anymore.

We often don't realize how much work we initially put into, nor do we recognize why romance is essential in marriage, and how a lack of romance can lead to an emotional meltdown and stagnation.

Romance generally includes one or more of:

1. Small actions which transmit affection, praise, sincerity, and love

2. Activities or acts of novelty-actions carried out for no reason other than to maximize feelings of joy and attachment

3. Class – operations or events that add a touch of an elevated life.

4. Any actions that bring a couple closer, or show consideration and affection

There are couples who still find it difficult with the idea of how to be affectionate in a relationship, decades after marriage. It's easy to create romance in a relationship when you become aware of the following:

Linkage

It is created from experiences that bring partners closer together. This can be accomplished by acts of affection, gift-giving, remembrance, meaningful conversation, excitement, and Intimacy.

Pleasure

Romance should be a happy experience; and is often reflected by enjoyable things such as going to the cinema, the festival, hosting parties together, or playing games.

Nostalgia

Being together for a long time, couples can share memories through a reflection on the past. Going through old photographs or revisiting past hang-out spots can bring back old feelings and thus boost bonds.

Humor

Humor is an essential element of most romantic love. Couples with a great sense of humor will love childish adornments, humorous greeting cards, comics, and the ridiculous chuckle.

Intercourse

Romance, sex, and relationships all go hand in hand, and sex is integral to his health in romantic relationships.

It will certainly increase passion by introducing new concepts into the sex life, or simply by engaging in sexual activities more often. Though romance can offer rise to Intimacy, Intimacy and romance can fuel each other.

Thrill

Spontaneity — from the normal activities that promote a spirit of adventure, such as walking together in the woods, getting "lost" on a drive, or doing something taboo — like going to visit an adult book store — is a great way to create romance through adventure.

6.4 Fun, Cheap, and Creative Date Ideas

Head on a Picnic

That's such an easy, yet a pleasant way to just hang out together! Sometimes, instead of loading all our food, we'll grab a pizza from a Domino or some subs to change things up.

Then I just need to put a salad or some fruit together, and we have a simple, delicious meal! Because I prepare all our meals mostly from nothing, this is a huge pleasure for us!

Hang out at a Coffee Shop

Take a coffee (or smoothie, or chai!) and hang out to talk to the one you love.

This is particularly suitable for those dates where you like you have a lot of catch-ups to do or have specific things you want to explore together!

Go for a Hike

Trekking or hiking paths can be a fun way to spend time together, even if you're like us and aren't super outdoor! Several of my best memories of the date involve actual times when we did it.

Free Night in the Museum

Numerous museums and parks have free days where anybody can join them for free. Check to see when there are free days for tourist spots in your area and go and enjoy some local culture!

Go to a Bookstore

Most Barnes and Noble shops have spots where you can sit and read, and also usually have inside a Starbucks.

We love to browse for books, grab a dessert or drink to share and then sit down together and enjoy our books. We're both lovers of books, so this is our easy-to-do cheap favorite date.

Go Through old Photographs

Always enjoyable to have a trip down memory lane! Pull out old pictures from before you've been together and share your stories.

Or remember together your early years as you look at life-capturing pictures.

Completing a Puzzle Together

Turn on your favorite tunes, pick up a puzzle, and see how quickly you can work together to finish it off!

Go out for Some Dessert

I enjoy dining out, but it can get too costly so easily! So sometimes, instead, we will just go out for dessert.

It keeps things cheap but still lets us have the fun to eat out.

Go on a Drive

Jump into the vehicle, and discover a new location. Or simply enjoy the scenery in a rural locale.

Pop into your favorite CD or listen to an eBook together if you don't feel like talking too much.

Explore the City/Walk Around

Take a walk around the neighbourhood. Head to your city's new area, and have fun exploring! Of course, the only rule is that you must hold your hands! ☺

Do you want to render it more interesting? Seek to do a nature scavenger hunt alphabet when you're at it.

Conclusion

Passion is an essential part of Intimacy. It's the desire to move further, and the linking spark. Passion is usually second nature in romantic relationships early on; the new energy of the relationship perpetuates the momentum to explore. You are trying new things, and you are craving to find every nook and cranny of the body and soul of your partner. Some couples keep this longer than others, but in the end, we have to imagine new ways of connecting. Here are a few thoughts:

Discover love

What's turning you on? What are some fantasies you've had recently? How comfortable are you allowing your mind and body to sit in those fantasies and potentially new and appalling sources of excitement? Explore your body and think of ideas, pictures, and things that make you feel excited.

The Process of Expressing and Discussing Dreams Together is Relaxing

If you don't know what that appears like or give them a chance to understand, your partner can't be the sexual being of your dreams. Make a list of fantasies and share this with your companion, understanding that there is no judgment on either side or expectations.

Sex Positions

The Ultimate Guide for Beginners and Advanced Sex Positions to boost Pleasure in your Relationship, Discover a new Level of Intimacy and improve your Sex Life with Hot and Spicy Tips

By

Rachel Bell and Tony Bravo

The trademarks that are used are without any consent, and the publication of the trademark is without permission or backing by the trademark owner. All trademarks and brands within this book are for clarifying purposes only and are the owned by the owners themselves, not affiliated with this document.

Table Of Contents

Introduction

From missionary to doggy and the entirety in between, there are limitless positions that couples may also use to get down and to get dirty. Recent research suggests that a man's or a woman's preferred sex positions might also point out many things about his/her deeper personality.

In this book, we will discuss the sexual union and focus on desire stimulation, several extraordinary embraces, caressing forms, and kissing. It also contains specific strategies for mild bondage, such as scratching, biting, and slapping.

After the initial two chapters on the relationship between a man and a woman, the book describes sexual positions, movements, and actions, defining exceptional forms of sexual acts. You can discover a variety of intercourse positions ranging from effortless to very complex; in addition, we will provide some sexual education as well.

Developing a range of sexual positions no longer only provides lovemaking enchantment; however, it can also help resolve some problems. For example, the multiplied stimulation to the G-spot that happens when a man enters from behind his companion will help the female achieve orgasm faster.

We all know that some conditions occur, such as the man having a tiny penis, and the girl is unable to get that much pleasure. Or vise the other way around – when the man has a too huge penis, which makes the girl experience greater disagreeable than pleasure. But, luckily, with the help of some particular intercourse positions, such incompatibility can be effortlessly removed.

Once you are conscious of the sensitive sector and its particular position in the vagina, you will intentionally stimulate them, conveying the woman more than one orgasms.

Chapter 1: Complicity in Couples

Complicity, as simple as it would possibly be to say, wishes two accomplices. In a couple's workshop, a man was once heard pronouncing the following to a woman, "I can not have a connection to you on my own; you, yourself, have to be complicit in having a relationship with me, or this might not work."

1.1 The Significance of Couple Complicity

Complicity capability that all the events anticipate whole manipulate of their separate commitments to the relationship, which renders them collectively responsible for the well-being of the marriage, recognizing that any selections have taken one at a time or together, for precise or bad, have an effect on one another. It involves standing alongside one any other at exceptional instances and standing even nearer on difficult moments – in no way being absent when needed, whatever the reasons or instances – echoing the attitude, "Strong people upward jostle up for themselves; however, greater humans stand up for their primary others." Complicity is the focus that a scenario arises when a man and a girl recognize that their unique schemes can be satisfactorily achieved as a conspiracy. Complicity regularly signifies that the parties worried are dedicated to being absolutely compliant in their duties in the direction of every other, seeing that one's loyalty to a partnership depends on one's dedication to oneself.

When you are not totally worried about your personal life, you can't be entirely energetic in a partnership. The reward of complicity is no longer actual until it comes alongside with the actuality of who you are. An ancient expression stipulates, "Justice not only needs to be served but however, it also needs to be heard."

Similarly, with relationships, "Complicity must now not solely be done, but it needs to also be viewed to be accomplished." It has to also be performed in such a way that it is an apparent effort that is built on belief and deliberate-reflecting the mind-set "I am complicit with myself in complicity with you." If we do apprehend the complexities of reciprocity, the thought of being worried in a partnership takes on additional complexity.

Reciprocating in a positive way inside the framework of a partnership means "giving your associate as tons as your partner provides you in the spirit of prosperity," such that a structural discrepancy is not generated that one associate provides all and the different companion takes away. Reciprocity occurs as each party's give and takes in a manner that is regular overtime, and that leads to the desires and preferences of all people, respectively.

Reciprocity is a corollary to cooperation, which helps to support and enhance the relationship.

Exercised over months and years, it adds to the cohesive combination of personalities that make up the couple a rainbow of colors. Never be taken for granted, the couples revel in every other's contributions as a testimony to their rising affection. Let's now not remember that participation is not a static thing; as the couples grow and alter, it develops and improves. It is via yummy complicity that a couple can produce extra of the stuff they favor and much less of the factors they do not want. In a way, it is like they can tailor the partnership to become a representation of who they are and how they react to each other, collaborating collectively to put it to life. It relinquishes the concept of ever giving up on one another.

It is in the spirit of the wholeness produced in the relationship that the couples put into it, satirically composed of the individual components, that the threads of their needs weave the tapestry of their mutual life.

They, by no means, underestimate the ability of exquisite collaboration to adorn a friendship and decorate it.

"True love is a continuously evolving feeling."

The "self-expanding feeling" is driven via deception in the sense of long-term intimate partnerships, and it is a big difference that makes all the difference.

1.2 Common Couples Problems

- **Money**

Money enables me to put it up straight!

Money wars are in no way over cash among couples. So if you choose a foreign money dispute to be minimized, track it back to the uncertainty that drives it.

Instead of arguing for the sum of cash wasted on who-knows-what, concentrate on what definitely matters:

1. Your fear of no longer having manipulated on imperative matters influencing your life
2. Your worry of not having steadiness in your future
3. Your worry of now not having consideration for your beliefs
4. Your fear of struggling to fulfill your goals

- **Work**

For you, I have two words: date night. I do know. You realized this a thousand times: do a night time of a weekly date, or your family will fail. It sounds greater like a threat than the right guidance, isn't it? Yet it is a surefire potential of mitigating administrative center tension.

Despite this repeated advice, it does no longer seem like the message is getting through. How frequently married people, between a long time of 25 and 50 with two or extra children, have a date night, here:

- Four percentage once each week
- Monthly: 21 percent
- Once each and every 2-3 months: 21 percent
- 18 percentage about once four to six months
- Once in seven weeks or less frequently: 36 percent

Oops...! We can do better, and there is a right reason to do that. The University of Virginia's National Marriage Project currently released a document dubbed "The Date Night Chance." This research found that husbands and better halves who set apart a dedicated time to combine and have fun at least one time in a week were about three and a half times more likely to file being "really satisfied" in their marriages.

- **Sex**

I recommend focusing on solving "coordination failure" to keep sexual frustrations down and the marital bedsprings jumping. It is frequent trouble in marriages. The quantity one clarification couples mention now not getting sex in their marriage is "So busy," shortly accompanied by way of "Not in the mood." Much of the time, its slang, intentionally or not, for getting intercourse drives that have no longer lined up.

So, start to talk about it. I can almost see you cringing when I compose this. For most people, it's as convenient to think about sex as napping in a bed. Yet it's a dialog that is key to aligning the intercourse drives and removing disagreements. When the time is correct, once you are each comfortable and no longer blinded, ask each other to provide an explanation for when you're most keen to go to bed. You may be amazed to hear your answers.

- **Children**

The answer to nearly any parenting hostilities is to get on the same web page and to create a coherent front.

Otherwise, the youngsters are manipulating every other against you and adding warmness to the parental flames. Conflict is diminishing as coordination grows. It may now not be handy to agree with your spouse on the suggestions and norms you and your young people are inclined to enforce. That is why ironing out variations at the back of locked doorways is the first order of business.

Don't attempt to get to the bottom of your parenting squabbles right now — whilst the children enjoy the show. The second comes when the two of you are free to discuss your proposals and unravel trade-offs. Hold on collectively as soon as you attain an agreement. When dad and mom form a robust front, there may be no room for I-told-you-so recrimination.

- **Chores**

Let's face it — the bulk of housework wars show up when one companion holds track. That is a misconception. Marriage scales are continually in motion, and solely if you have a symbolic scoreboard constructed in your partnership, you are placing yourself up for trouble. Using the exchange division technique would do away with all that.

For example, Amanda is higher and quicker than Chris, each at making the dishes and at rearranging up round the house. She absolutely does it in half of the time it takes for him. Does it make the experience for Chris to do either of these tasks, given this fact? Not quite. That makes it feel it is for Chris to fill up their pet's water bowl and equip their kid's bedtime space. He organizes and video display units their budgets faster too. He is doing it in half of the time that Amanda would take. He's a form of precise at ironing his very own shirts as well.

You get the picture. It is pretty simple. Prevent attempting to divide up the center of the household tasks. Love is better lived when you don't attempt to balance out the scales.

Conflict is a truth of existence; however, no longer a terrible one. When you're your partner hitting it up next — and you are going to — go beforehand and battle it out, however, conflict it with the purpose of getting closer, perception him or her better, and loving each different well even in the center of discord.

1.3 What is your Sex Personality?

That's answerable in a cursory way by using what stirs you up. Consult the grownup television, look up the books, and see the responses. They are a suitable base from which to decipher your desires.

Nevertheless, you will want to do a little more than that to truly understand your feelings about the topic. You'll want to go out to do something for it, encouraging yourself to try and see the stuff you're concerned in. There is a way greater about recognizing yourself than simply what turns you on and is no longer going to be apparent unless you have the information of it.

Oddly enough, I just had spoken with any person who's just starting out on their day trip on this. On this topic, he has lots of expectations but no actual experience. With people establishing that journey, I locate that they frequently have certain misconceptions that can also affect the capability to identify their very own configuration and emotions that I generally strive to help them fix. Typically, I hear any of the following subsets:

- "You can both be dominant or submissive"—no, most folks are greater inclined than their equivalents to a mixture of one or the other. That's 99 percentage one way for positive individuals, one percentage the other direction, but don't pursue self-discovery besides exploring options in your orientation or you're no longer going to find out anything.

- "You'll simply know"—maybe, however, most of the human beings I've spoken to nonetheless want the experience to locate out the finer small print and where they had been inclined to contradict their self-image (particularly with woman dominants or male submissive), it commonly takes a little time to sort out the variance between what they felt they were supposed to experience and what they surely felt.

- "There is solely one proper capacity of becoming aggressive or submissive"—no, there are very, very unique patterns of a role, function orientations, and play values. Look for the direction that appears correct to you inner the strictures of consent.

- "It'll look like it is in the movies"—no and hell no. The media does a terrible job of presenting partnerships in BDSM. Don't search for something that resembles a video you've watched or a novel you've got read. Look for yourself to feel it when having to effect something dictated via people who have no understanding of what BDSM is.

- "You've acquired to do matters correctly otherwise you're not dominant/submissive"—BDSM is ... well, it is perhaps better to communicate about it as a talent in any other case artwork style. You learn you boost expertise and your goal for some kind of collaborative performance. Whether or no longer your personality is most efficient or submissive does not hold on to excellence, however, on the traits that evolve with time through study and capacity learning.

- "You've acquired to be some form of a person,"-nope. There are aged people, youth, skinny people, overweight people, suit men, couch potatoes, human beings of all ethnicity and financial backgrounds, and us who exercise or engage in the BDSM. The films may also treat BDSM like it has a face, but you do not have to personalize a leather outfit or be a model to officially 'be' in BDSM, in all seriousness.

I'd inform you now not to be nervous. However, I find a lot of people anxious about it. Instead, I would suggest you be open-minded and equipped to explore the topic. That has to tell you what you're into pretty quickly.

Chapter 2: Understanding the Sexual Desires

Do you consider when you were the first beginning relationship with your wife? Remember the joy you felt, emotionally, and physically? So when you, in reality, went to mattress together, oh, are you nevertheless blushed from experience? Were these your glory times of Sex — when romantic love used to be energetic, intense, and you could not wait to go to bed?

But now, after six years, possibly a child, and a mortgage, led to a change in things? You've probably changed. Your husband will indeed be joyful to have Sex as a good deal as he shaves, but it may have been one more significant item on the to-do listing for you. If you are having Sex as soon as a week, heck, you're happy, even once every two weeks.

2.1 Understanding Sexual Needs

You might also be changing, and you and he may also be having some differences. One way of bringing things into context is to discuss how you and your associate may additionally range in some ways. Every weekend, he likes to play golf; you'll as an alternative curl up with a book. Every night, you may have ice cream; however, he is at ease once in a month with it. Get the idea? As in many cases, when it comes to particular intercourse desires, you are special.

The trouble is that there might be something more going on. After all, riding is solely a phase of what makes desire. Another just-as-important phase is motivation.

Psychological and interpersonal elements that create a dedication or hobby to be sexual with your associate are reflected in motivation.

For example, some studies advise that if one associate in a marriage has a low sex drive, unconsciously "withholding" Sex could be an ability to gain management in the relationship. That is a reason, albeit one focused on Sex. Or it may additionally be a technique to show your sadness regarding the partnership. In other words, if you are unhappy with your relationship, there is no hobby in having Sex with any individual you're no longer completely happy with outside the bedroom.

Still, in the partnership, let's say you are satisfied. Say you love your partner really, and you truly prefer your sex force to be as driven. Just now, you do not have the motivation to get it there.

Following are some methods that can assist you re-ignite your passion:

- Sit back, and speak freely and frankly about the sex drive discrepancies. Speaking about the problems will assist beautify trust and contact.
- Tell your hubby/partner/lover that you can not reciprocate as often; however, you are flattered by means of an obvious sexual desire for you, and your love is strong.
- Clarify to the associate that telling "no tonight's no longer the night time is now not a personal denial. You claim no because of a sex enchantment discrepancy — a discrepancy of desire.
- Work as a group to alleviate your defensiveness and settle your disagreements over how plenty you want Sex.
- Aim for agreement. So, for starters, if your spouse wants Sex five days a week, and you desire Sex once a week (or less), possibly consider getting Sex for a while twice a week.

- Plan sex, an awful lot like you would like time table a pedicure or haircut. You are, at the identical time, setting yourself in a physical nation of mind with the aid of bringing in Sex and spending the days prior to the "appointment," wondering about it.

Get some other sit-down to discuss with your wife after a month. How are matters going on? Does your associate experience more physically content? Do you sense connected? Would you two virtually like the lovemaking?

If so, it can be time to step it on to the next stage. Start by way of having another "sex date." Because that is the thing: the extra often you make love, the extra you would possibly want to make love!

But, what if the reverse happens? Instead of wanting to have Sex more frequently, you locate your urge hasn't clearly shifted, and you just don't favor making love despite a couple of weeks' effort — now not even twice a week. Now it is time to make sacrifices for your partner.

You'll be the initiator for the subsequent month, for example. You both agree that when you provoke it, you will solely have Intercourse. See how that goes, and add up how regularly you have had Sex after a month. Ask how you all feel. If either of you felt that the amount of intimacy was once troubling, it really is when it is time for an expert consult.

Begin with your health care professional to make positive nothing else is medically wrong; then think about meeting with an intercourse therapist.

And notice, Sex itself is no longer the most essential thing of any sexually-related issue, however how you talk about Intercourse and your personal wishes and satisfaction.

2.2 Quiz for Understanding Sexual Desires

1- How a great deal would you have desired to participate in physical contact with an accomplice in this remaining month (e.g., rubbing one another's genitals, providing or obtaining oral pleasure, Intercourse, etc.)?

    A. Not at all

    B. Once a month

    C. Once every week

    D. Once every two weeks

2- How regularly did you have sexual ideas involving a companion over this closing month?

    A. Not at all

    B. Once a month

    C. Once each and every week

    D. Once every two weeks

3- How effective is your urge to simply take part in bodily Intercourse with a partner while you have sexual thoughts?

    A. Actually, I'm now not very fascinated with this

    B. If my companion had been here, I would probably go for it

    C. I ought to take it or pass on it

    D. I do wish my partner had been right here and we could get going

4- How powerful is your capacity to act on it when you see a human you consider sexually attractive?

    A. I sincerely do not sense any sexual desire

    B. I will think about it on and off for a day or two

    C. I might assume about Sex fleetingly; however, it rapidly disappears

    D. I will regularly fantasize about the individual and on occasion masturbate wondering about them

5- How effective is your sexual desire when you are in romantic conditions (such as a candle light dinner, or a walk along the beach, etc.)?

  A. I like the romance; however, I don't specifically favor Sex
  B. I get turned on and hope it will lead to a sexual encounter

6- How would you rate your capacity to act sexually with a mate, in contrast to different humans of your age?

  A. Very low
  B. I suppose I am in all likelihood about the equal as other people
  C. Maybe a bit lower than others
  D. I assume I'm greater involved in Sex

7- How frequently have you masturbated at some point in the closing two months (including touching your genitals for enjoyment, inserting something into your vagina, or making an attempt to get an orgasm)?

  A. Not at all
  B. Once a month
  C. Once every week
  D. Once each two weeks

8- How powerful is the urge to expose yourself to sexual behavior?

  A. I by no means assume about masturbating or touching myself pleasurably
  B. I suppose about masturbating quite a lot

9- How lengthy can you go effortlessly without having any type of sexual activity, both on your own or with a partner?

  A. Probably a year
  B. Maybe a few months
  C. About a month
  D. No longer than two weeks

10- When I watch an attractive video or read an attractive novel, I...!

A. Skip via the sex scenes--I suppose they are boring
B. I have a fleeting feeling of growing to become on; however, it doesn't last
C. I find them exciting to read; however, they don't turn me on
D. I get grew to become one, and I like to revisit those scenes to flip myself on more at different instances

2.3 How should you Dress to Increase Excitement?

So my wife and I went and purchased new cotton panties, which I viewed a little greater eye-catching in which we ought to each be satisfied. It is essential that what you purchase and put on suits excellent with you. And if you have body issues (most of us do!) are searching for to put them at the door whilst reading how to gown sexily. That's notably obvious; however, I have to say it to make certain I drive home the point: buy and put on garments that highlight matters you both love about your body, whether or not it's your breasts, your legs, or even your back; something that makes you experience sexy. Your man would love the dedication that you are giving to him, and his confident emotions would help you shine.

- **In the Bedroom**

Casual

Minimal make-up and clothing with small efforts, such as a pair of bootie shorts or one of his gown shirts. Throwing on a pair of heels transforms nearly any seem to be; you would possibly use day by day into a provocative "sexy feel." With his loved shorts and bra, you can notice that simply strutting about nonchalantly, would seriously change his eye.

Lingerie

Moderate make-up, in some way elegant hair (looking for a put-together look), and an extensive range of lingerie, lengthy and silky, or brilliant and tight, or lacy and girly, etc. Putting on the closing touches like shoes and stockings can decorate the feel.

Dress-up

Suitable make-up for your theme (e.g., minimal and harmless for "school girl" versus "escort" dark and slutty), as nicely as correct styled hair ... faculty women normally come with pig-tails! There is a number of frequent styles that you might costume up in, but right here, you additionally favor adding a lot of diversity.

Props

One way to enhance your "sexy feel" except making an attempt to consist of a particular vogue is via wearing one-piece fishnet outfits, a lot more erotic than lingerie. And shoes, of course!

Wearing nothing but a thong and those thigh-high boots is a look of its own way. While the top brought through your heels can decorate these sex positions, be careful: I have nearly gouged my husband with my preferred stilettos countless times!

Outside the House

Discretion is crucial. Taking into account where you journey and what you are going to do. When you have dinner with his boss, an outfit that may additionally be warm for a night out dancing collectively might not appear sexy. Yet there's continually plenty of chances to wear & seem good!

If you're wearing a satisfactory dress or skirt for nighttime out, amp up the heat by means of leaving your panties behind. This one is a bit of fun when you're at home, but a lot of fun when you are away from home. It matches especially properly if the nighttime involves a chance for him to slip a hand up your leg (like the movies), and it would not work if you're somewhere it might make him experience uncomfortable (like dinner in the residence of his parents!).

2.4 Most Common Error in Dressing for Him and for Her

- **Mistakes via Him**

So awesome even I had one in 1991. I used to rock it out in my Fun Jeans / Cross Colors. This crew is now not limited to shark tooth necklaces but includes all devices putting from the neck that are innovative or influenced by way of nature. Keep it ultra-simple if you want to put on jewelry-either don't put on any or take a look at out a man referred to as Johnny Ramli.

I mustn't have to bang about this; however, guys don't listen. You can never wear white socks with a swimsuit or dark denim and boots until you are in a hurry to attain a happy hour or stand in line for a spit roast. It is like driving while drunk; please don't. Get a cab, take black socks, and get serious.

No, no, no, and a little greater no. I do not care what swimsuit company you are buying, or even if it's your dad's, you have to have a suit constantly; it is tailored to fit you. You want to appreciate the fit, no count, whether you are slim or a little portly. Keep in mind; you have to feel like a King in a suit.

I can not say that in my life, I noticed a lot of bad underwear; however, I realize it's out there. If it is on the internet, then you purchase it.

It is additionally vital to word that undergarments have a shelf-life. It's excellent to transfer them to the big underwear draw in the sky as quickly as you see moderate wear, smudges, or a funky odor. Underwear is cheap, so make a suitable investment.

- **Mistakes via Her**

You have to sense comfortable at the give up of the day. If you can't relax in your new corset or your new footwear are apt to sprain afoot, then your glamorous gown won't carry too lots of spice to your intercourse life.

Consider being as daring as you can. But if you don't sense very comfortable, here's a tip: Hold the lighting down the first time you put on a new horny outfit for your guy. Just take note that pitch black isn't always going to work, because if he cannot see your gown and you can't see his reaction, you are kind of defeating the aim.

In addition to convenience, seek to bear in the idea that your outfit is accessible. Unless you're experienced making an attempt new outfits together, do your nice to keep away from something that will take you greater than five minutes to get out of to have terrific instances together anything longer can truly kill the mood.

Don't spend too long getting prepared. My husband and I experimented with role-playing for the first time, it was once necessary to me to get dressed up and feel as sexy as feasible in order to without a doubt take on my part. After an hour of applying (and reapplying) make-up to pose like an escort and another 1/2 hour of choosing the proper jacket, coat, coordinating nylons with no gaps and socks, I came out to see him almost asleep on the sofa.

Now every time my wife needs to seem to be and feel good, and she attempts to get ready in boost with the aid of making positive that she is freshly showered and washed and that her hair is curled. She likes to be simply conscious of how she is doing her make-up, improving elements but now not being passed over too closely except the state of affairs demands it. Early on, she puts on her ideal outfit to make sure she won't fight for a misplaced belt or string ultimate minute, and love feeling attractive as properly as imagining the smile on my face and the attainable suitable instances later on.

If you're cozy and open to new ideas, he likes it when it comes to dressing up horny for your man, then attempts to have a variety of horny appears from casual and subtle to warm and racy. This way, you may be able to hold your guy's excessive degree of sexual interest and wish for quite a whole lot ever.

- **Keep in Mind**

Men are very visible creatures, and if there may be one component that's sexier than you have dressed up in something hot for your partner, it is that layer of self-confidence you are going to wear when you experience attractive and choose to show it.

2.5 Most Common Mistakes Regarding Sex

- **Mistakes Women Make**

Not making an effort to Initiate Sex

Most of us are worried about involving ladylike conduct. For fear of being considered rude, we don't want to seem pushy or come on too hard. It is one of the best mistakes girls make when they refuse to initiate Intercourse.

Most guys experience like they're continuing the initiator, and this causes a difference in the partnership on the intensity scale, "he notes. Men commonly choose to be approached just as much with the aid of their companions as women do.

Holding onto old notions about sex roles additionally prevents pride in our sexual relationships. They used to consider ladies are less involved in sexual activity, and I no longer desire to say that. I think women are as interested in Sex [as men].

Show your hobby from time to time by using taking the first step. Your husband would, in reality, revel in it, and you can experience a new degree of achievement in taking credit score for your sexual relationship.

Worrying What You Look Like

Starting to think about how you seem all through Sex will stop you from appreciating yourself, and will break your chances of orgasm.

"Don't think of the fats on your stomach or make-up on your face." Focus on the pleasure of performing. You have to encourage yourself to have an orgasm.

"Males favor their better halves to provide up in sex play, and it is no longer probably if she's anxious related to her physical concerns.

Men do not observe 1/2 the things females obsess about anyway.

"It's awesome what men do not notice when you're passionate, full of energy, engaged in them, and flexible."

There is an evolutionary rationalization of our bodily flaws for the selective blindness guys show. People are looking out (unknowingly, of course) of females who can elevate nutritious children. Beginning hundreds and thousands of years ago, there lived on people who drew fertile females and had various babies — the ones who couldn't have died out. While perhaps not as vital today, the primitive method for survival lives on.

"Men are drawn even more to girls who display signs of health and vitality and fertility. Instead of wondering about your waist and hip appearance, think about your degree of energy, and your passion and self-assurance in it, "Fisher suggests.

Sex is an Informal Issue for the Men

We should all let go of old school ideologies, for example, that ladies are not intimate or that Sex is simply Sex for men. "Sex is a surely necessary undertaking for some men. Do now not downplay it.

The research helps the concept that, in the experience of a committed relationship, both guys and girls locate sexual intimacy extra satisfying.

"Numerous statistical surveys make it pretty evident that married partners are the humans who have the perfect content and the most energetic Sex. That says a lot about 'casual sex' failings.

The figures show that guys are simply as concerned about Sex and relationships as women. In fact, above 50 percentage of females and 52 percent of men who entered a one-night stand published that they did so in the hope of developing a long relationship. In fact, one-third of them did so. What can we learn?

"Never presume a man is not romantic." Two foremost blunders in this subculture are that girls are no longer sexual and that men are now not as intimate [as women].

Thinking that He is constantly up for the Sex

Sure, younger most teenagers are inclined and ready on every occasion you ask, but no longer authentic of men. Everyday life's pressures — family, work, bills — may additionally zap a man's libido. This comes to a lot of us as a big shock, and once in a while, his lack of involvement in Sex is something we take personally.

"It comes as such a shock that [women] clearly don't accept it," Fisher says of the response that many girls have when their husband suggests they're no longer in a temper for Intercourse. "They comprehend that they don't frequently have an interest in Sex; however, they always love the guy. But when they find out that he does not prefer Sex, they say, 'he doesn't prefer me.' Not true. He simply doesn't prefer to have Sex.'

Not providing him Guidance

We might also sense uncomfortable speaking definitely openly about Sex, what we like and don't like, even with an individual we have been with for a long duration of time and otherwise experience close to. But this is the only way to accomplish fulfilling sexual Intercourse.

"A female has to endure responsibility for her sexual experience." No man can get a female to orgasm until she accepts responsibility for her sexual encounter. Even the fine lover can not understand what she desires besides letting him know.

The desirable news is guys want to please girls very much.

"When you can reassure them in a manner that does not harm their pride, they can understand.

She recommends women to sandwich what they do now, not like between 5 things due to the fact he is listening. "You're no longer going to discover out until you're in mattress with him next time. But guys are listening, specifically, if you are quite clear on that.

When he suggests something new, you get upset

It's ordinary to want to spice matters up with a little variant after a pair have been collectively for a while. Only because your man likes to attempt something new does no longer mean that he or she is sad with you or with your sex life. In short: Don't idea it.

Still, it is necessary to tune in your alleviation zone.

"Nobody should ever experience obliged to do something in the intimate and non-public place of sexuality they don't desire to do." If your man desires you to do anything past your morals, make it known that it is off your boundaries, and justify why. Do so in a caring way as best you may, of course. If it's something about you that isn't always even an ethical problem, however, you by some means do not desire to, then make clear that again. If it's, in reality, a stunning request and you are uncomfortable about it at first, attempt not to react negatively. Let him know, instead, that you want some time to assume about it.

- **Mistakes Men Make**

Sex Starts Off-Evolved inside the Bedroom

Guys may also flip on like a light; however, arousal doesn't appear so shortly for women.

Pave the way via cuddling, kissing, and retaining arms in the course of the daytime. Have exciting together, and exhibit her that you respect her.

Feeling cozy and confident in the partnership is essential to let a woman free for the duration of Intercourse virtually. A deep hug can go in addition to you would have thought. "Hugging for 30 seconds prompts oxytocin, the feminine hormone that produces a feeling of attachment and trust."

Suppose you be Aware of what She Desires

Today, as many ladies pretend orgasms as they did 20 or 30 years ago. And if she does not experience herself, you probably may not know.

Don't worry about asking questions like "How does this feel?" Or "Do you like anything different?" To put it another way, ask for instructions.

Stay with the Strategy

Don't think "if it worked the first three times, it's going to work the subsequent three times.

It can depend on her temper concerning what turns her on, and where she is in her monthly period. "Maybe her nipples are extra sensitive, or her genitals are less tingly.

Pay heed to your companion. "Try number stuff to see how she's coping."

Keep it "Extremely Physical"

Expand the foreplay idea. Some human beings "concentrate on bodily stimuli and often overlook mental stimulus.

While guys get sparked with the aid of what they see, "females fantasize a lot as part of [the] arousal manner for the duration of sex."

Expect her to have an Orgasm for the Duration of Intercourse

Sex alone will no longer do the job for eighty percent of women. Why not? Most sex positions do no longer assist prompt the clitoris directly.

There are other ways to fulfill her. "Women climax from oral Intercourse even more frequently than from Intercourse. Also, consider Sex with the woman on top, or a vibrator designed to use by partners all through sleep. "Men need to experience relaxed, no longer intimidated, with intercourse toys.

To make her hit the candy word when you have Sex, take time to allow her to get started out before you move in. "The nearer women are as they provoke Intercourse, the more likely they can get an orgasm.

Do no Longer attempt Seduction

Women enjoy being seduced. "Seduction is as important as, or at instances more critical than, approach.

Whether it's oral, visual, or psychological, she says, it helps recognize what sort of turn-on your companion wants. "When you discuss dirty over the mobile or the text, does your associate like it? Track your finger up the chest slowly? Flirt at a pub with her?

Also, if you like whatever you see, just say so? "Let a female recognize how acceptable she is.

Concentrate on Ringing the Bell

Most girls tend to get an orgasm from the clitoral stimulation; however, it is more elaborate than you would expect.

Some men "don't apprehend the clitoris anatomy. It's more than the tiny "button" you can see. Its nerve fibers unfold across the vulva and inner the vagina. It's all doubtlessly worth exploring for pleasure.

You pass back and forth. It will steal away certain women's enjoyment by way of paying such close attention to the glans at the top of the vulva. It's so delicate that an awful lot of pressure will hurt.

Chapter 3: Some must try Sexual Positions

3.1 Spooning Positions

- **"69" - The Role of Mutual Sucking**

The "69" role is where one lover is lying head to tail over the other, and each gives simultaneous oral stimulation to the other.

Oral stimulation in this role can work effortlessly if its mouth is extensive sufficient for its penis and if it is now not aggressively thrusting.

Engorging the erectile penis in her mouth, she grabs his testicles and caresses them, permitting her saliva to pour over them.

Pressing her buttocks' cheeks apart, the man will caress her vulva's widely unfold lips at his amusement with the tip of his tongue, titillating her anus with his tongue as well. He may want to stimulate her clitoris, as well.

If you're a man or woman who loves to lick and explore the genitals with the tongue, then this can be a very thrilling route to orgasm at the identical time.

- **"Penetrating the Eye" Position**

Holding his member higher tightly with her buttocks in the opening and - to underline his superiority-smacking her on the bottom and rubbing it heat with one hand, he holds her clitoris with the other, his lover being unable to withstand his caresses. The joy and enjoyment gesture appreciably accentuates the man's wish so that when she feels his lover is close to ejaculatory orgasm, the woman has to pause.

Then the man still lodged on the mattress kneels in the woman's bottom. His spouse sits up, with her breasts touching his face. He massages her labia and clitoris with one hand and can even masturbate her if he thinks her pelvic motions are extreme enough. He rubs her breasts with a different hand, which has grown erectile from his interesting caresses, whilst his fingertips make investments their genitals.

3.2 Standing Positions

- **"Climbing the Tree" Position**

It is one of the Kama Sutra's most endearing and most gratifying places. The woman standing subsequent to the man swaddle her legs spread greater or much less high round him as if she were to climb a tree with the exception that as a steady branch, she makes use of her penis to avoid her falling.

The enthusiasts face each different so they can share all kinds of caresses, pinching so kissing each other, they appear reflecting their mounting desire reciprocally.

This role is very precise for increasing the strength of intercourse along the spine. The fanatics can have exceptional orgasms depending on the degree they carry the sexual anxiety at.

- **The Gazelle and the Stallion" Position**

This role offers the lady the extremely good gain of inducing severe vaginal sensations.

The top area of the vagina is additionally very a great deal encouraged through the horizontally inserted glans and penis shaft. In order to accentuate this rubdown even further, the girl permits her head to fall down to the floor and, nevertheless protecting on the wrists of her lover. With her buttocks lying on his thighs, she takes up her penis, which holds her balance greedily for the complete length of it.

This role helps females to have extra control over pleasure, as the sexual strength flows to the head along the spine, producing a multiplied orgasm type.

The man's standing posture permits him extra control over the level of gratification to prevent an ejaculatory orgasm.

- **"The Door AJAR" Position**

The man contains his lover by using the shoulders, then takes one of his lover's legs and gently pulls it down. The woman, turning barely to the side, reaches around the neck of her lover so as no longer to lose any of the penis' length. In this position, the vulva is now moisturized, well-lubricated from this position, allowing the penis to cross quickly, massaging the vagina's sides.

Both lovers should core their interest in the center of their foreheads to break out the man's ejaculatory orgasm and the explosive orgasm of the woman. In this way, they are more aware of the sexual force.

- **"Climbing the Tree" Position - Variant 1**

This is one of Kama Sutra's most lovable positions. The female standing next to the man swaddles her legs spread more or less excessive round him as if she has been to climb a tree with the exception that as a strong branch, she uses her penis to keep away from her falling.

The woman then placed one of her legs down, inserting it between her lover's thighs. The girl can elevate the different legs around the waist of the man, or if she has adequate suppleness, she can put it on his back.

This role demands that the fans honestly have the same top to do it.

The fanatics face each different so they can share all manner of caresses, pinching so kissing each other, their eyes reflecting their mounting desire reciprocally.

This model of the posture "Climbing the tree" is an ideal location to control the sexual energy. The standing positions generally amplify the energy of impact over the energies. The lovers will have unique orgasms relying on the diploma they carry the sexual anxiety at.

- **"Climbing the Tree" position - Variant 2**

This is some other version of Kama Sutra's loveliest place. The man standing before the lady raises her, so her vulva blends into his penis.

She wraps her legs extra or much less stretched around him, while her virile companion slips deep into her moist vagina.

Holding her thighs, he pulls her pelvis towards him, fully filling up her vagina.

The fanatics face each different so they can share caresses of all sorts, poke every other, and kiss each other. They will glimpse every different full of want and, as a consequence, mount their love.

This "Climbing the tree" posture variant is a very desirable role for man's management of sexual energy, as the standing role will increase the manipulate strength over the energies. The vertical area of the woman's trunk additionally lets in for better manipulate of her sexual resources. Lovers should center of attention their interest in the crown to sublimate the sexual energy in extra focused energies and thereby attain more and greater multiplied states of consciousness.

3.3 Woman on Top

- **"Penetration with Deep Backward Movement" - Variant**

The enthusiasts are positioning themselves in such a way that his member is guided from the rear to her buttocks.

He pulls her hip up to the stage of his waist when he inserts a hidden penis into the vulva of the girl and, at the identical time, forces her to tilt the top phase of her physique forward.

She supports herself on the ankles of her lover to maintain a higher balance so that he can convey his full energy to her. The way the penis massages the vagina and the vulva sucks the penis gives the pair a deep feeling of craving in this area of massage.

To preserve this position, the man would have sturdy muscles in his palms and legs as long as it is crucial to get the non-ejaculatory orgasm.

The girl in this scenario has a robust manipulate of the electricity of gratification, and so she can guide the man by way of stopping the movement when she feels he is attaining the pre-orgasmic level.

- **"Sucking and Massaging on the Mast" Function**

There are three resting positions for the man in Kama Sutra, whose difficult and wide member is skilfully massaged with the aid of the woman from the front from time to time and became to him on occasion with her back. One of them is the "massage and suck on the mast" role.

After one or two hours of sexual continence intercourse, the man can also take this position to relax and regain his vigor. The two fans exchange positions in this situation, the girl will become active, and the man turns into passive.

The lady lets the penis of her husband slip into her bloated, wet, and sparkling vagina. They can also either make motions up and down or repetitive motions. She has to give up her movement when she is aware that her lover is shut to the ejaculatory orgasm. To stop the ejaculatory orgasm of man and the explosive orgasm of women, both fans need to direct their sexual energy alongside the spine towards the crown.

Once she thinks her lover regains manipulate over the sexual force, the woman will restart her movements.

- **"Blows of the Planting Pin" Position**

Here is another so-called resting role for the man, whose girl skillfully massages erect member from the front.

After one or two hours of sexual continence intercourse, the man will take the position to relax and regain his vigor. The two enthusiasts share their roles in this position; the female becomes aggressive, and the man turns into passive. The lady impales on a difficult member of the family. She rocks again and forth and, for that reason, controls the penetration depth.

Holding her breasts, the man has to pull her pelvis towards him, making her push her penis to the hilt. She can play for all her length, and when her penis is entirely inner her, she can feel her pubic hair and scrotum on her vulva's lips, which in this role are wide open.

The lady lets the penis of her husband slip into her bloated, wet, and sparkling vagina. When she feels her lover is approaching the ejaculatory orgasm, she has to quit her moving.

To produce the sexual strength in pure passion, each lover needs to center of attention on their interest in the navel area.

- **"Sucking and Massage on the Mast" Position - Variant 1**

Here's some other so-called resting position for the guy whose lady skillfully massages the tough and massive member.

The man is no longer going. The female extends herself to the complete size of the penis, helping herself on her knees. If he feels more delight in this place, the man can unfold his legs. Sitting barely opposite the thighs of the man, the girl receives the phallus of the man to the diploma she chooses.

If she locates her pelvis on him, the man can keep her hips and assist her, or he can touch her buttocks with his arms with the fingers spread out. Such flicks assist the girl in increasing her sexual strength along the backbone.

For the beginners, in the artwork of lovemaking with the potential to control sexual movements, this role is encouraged as it helps sublimate the sexual electricity in more subtle energy. All fans have to pay attention to their interest in the core of their foreheads to direct the sexual power towards the sixth chakra-Ajna Chakra. They'll feel inner peace and joy in this way.

- **"Sucking and Massaging on the Mast" Function - Variant 2**

There is some other position for the man from inside the context of the so-called resting positions.

The guy is now not going. The girl puts the whole length of the penis in her wet womb, supporting herself on her legs and thighs of her husband, taking the lively role.

In that role, the girl just takes the phallus of the man to the extent she wants. After one or two hours of sexual continence intercourse, the man will take the position to rest and regain his vigor.

The man can nibble and pinch his lover's nipples, taking benefit of his position. They share caresses and kisses and see every difference as their exhilaration grows.

The girl lets the penis of her husband slip into her bloated, wet, and sparkling vagina. They might also make either move up and down or circular motions. If she thinks her lover is getting close to the ejaculatory orgasm, she has to interrupt her movement. All lovers need to direct their sexual strength toward the crown along the neck, to get away the ejaculatory orgasm of man and the explosive orgasm of woman.

Once she thinks that her lover has regained manipulate over the sexual energy, the girl will restart her movements.

3.4 Man on Top

- **"The Blow of the Bull" Role**

The man's penis actually covers the woman's obvious vulva. Her thighs are up to the degree of the man's shoulders, who plunges deeply and forcefully into her so she can experience his member's dimension and length all the better.

The lady can stroke the man's buttocks with her fingers all through "The Bull's Blast" phase.

The full of life thrusts of the man figure out the growing sexual strength of the lady alongside the spine.

- **"The Concealed Door" Role**

The man lies to his wife. She holds his legs, equipped to take him up to the hilt. He insinuates himself softly and profoundly rooted internal of her, cuddling her there, stroking her back, thighs, breasts. She stretches her legs and opens them barely to yield herself to the wants of her lover even in addition so that she can give her vulva to the glans and penis shaft fully.

Even in the same role, the male lover can also have enjoyable with his lover's anal opening, if he knows she loves anal penetrations. In this way, the woman can loosen up in the first-rate possible way, and the man has complete manipulate over his penis' penetration into the moist and confined opening that she gives him with love and trust. He holds her by her thighs, can bite her throat, and brush over her breasts with his hands, whilst thrusting ever deeper. The man's urge is entire in both cases and of a lengthy length.

This position is sufficient to bring up the sexual strength and sublimate it in pure love. To acquire this extended emotion-pure love, the enthusiasts do not have to focal point on the genital gratification throughout this phase. Still, they have to center of attention their attention on the region of the coronary heart and turn out to be aware of the flying feeling this segment creates. When the fans abandon them to the flying feeling, they like they're lost in an ocean of pure love.

- **"The Cares of the BUD" Function**

Lying on the floor, legs interlacing, the man and woman flip to every other with their backs. However, for certain men, whose brief and thick penis can solely be flexed with difficulty, the specific effect of this role can be incredibly painful. In the continuation of this role, the woman, who now retains her balance with one arm going through her lover and who is supported on the physique of the man, is solely titillated by means of the glans at the entrance of her vagina.

It is, of course, simply foreplay to deeper coitus. The guy inserts his erect penis into the vagina by using softly shifting to one side. Now the vagina is geared up to acquire it in full.

The function is suitable for these fanatics who are beginners in the art of regulating sexual energy. "The caress of the bud" position provides lovers with the opportunity of becoming more aware of the degree of gratification and, as a consequence, it through stopping the movement when they experience that they are shut to the climax.

They have to focal point their heed in the center of their brow for the sublimation of sexual energy. This will trigger a clear-minded state in both lovers, which will help them modify and sublimate the sexual power in higher energies.

- **"Face to Face"**

Holding on her arms and soles, the female raises her pelvis to allow the man to insert his penis into her vagina. Being kneeled, he may seize his lover's waist with one or both hands. This position helps lovers to seem at one another-seeing how their appeal rises and sharing their love.

The female should shift her pelvis softly, matching her step with the coming and going of the man's movements. To take up the full erectile length of her lover's cock, she has to unfold more often than not her legs.

If the man feels close to the ejaculatory orgasm, he has to end shifting and center of attention his interest in the location of the heart to sublimate the sexual energy. This can be achieved for the girl too.

- **"Driving the Nail Home" Position**

Facing her, with his chest pushing on her breasts, the man plunges into the vagina of the girl with full loins thrusts.

The female receives him with broadly unfold thighs right up to the hilt.

This role favors the entire intimacy of the lovers' genital zones.

Even if there is consistency between the dimension of the woman's vagina and the dimension of the man's penis, then the woman will attain the cervical-uterine orgasm that is usually for the tantric orgasm. Contrary to all assumptions, the female in this function needs to no longer be passive.

She has to hold close the man's buttocks and press his pelvis on hers to assist him in reaching deep into her.

This position in the art of sexual continence is now not recommended for beginners in view that it encourages the awareness of sexual energy in the genital region.

This is why the man must make slow movements and middle his interest in the cardiac plexus to adjust the sexual strength and give up the ejaculation.

- **"The Open Pincer" Role**

This is one of the submissions roles that is most fulfilled for an individual. On her back, the female spreads her legs. Her husband grips her knees, and she's pressured to unfold her legs even further. Having her legs spread like this, she can in no way fight against his invasion.

He can explore her to the content of his core-gently with the complete length of his penis or-which will stimulate her urge for food for more-he can aggressively insert and withdraw his member.

Both lovers ought to pay attention to their attention all through the "Open Pincer" position to direct the fundamental and sexual strength alongside the spine till the crown.

- **"The TOP" Position**

"The location of the TOP," being very similar to the missionary position, additionally known as "Driving the nail home" in Kama Sutra, makes it handy for the man to enter it without having to withdraw his penis from the vagina of his lover. That is why the fanatics would take the "top" role after the classical one to remain in contact with their genitals.

Tantric masters propose that fans keep in touch with their sexual organs at some point in intercourse, seeing that the intense interplay between fanatics that is initiated throughout the erotic act is no longer disrupted this way.

Within that role, the lady should now not be passive. Through preserving the thighs of the man, she will press his pelvis on hers, supporting him penetrate deeply into her.

Similar to the position of "Moving the nail home," "The peak" role in the art of sexual continence is not endorsed for beginners as it encourages the concentration of sexual power in the genital region. This is why the man must make gradual movements and middle his attention in the cardiac plexus to regulate the sexual electricity and end the ejaculation—recommended for kids, too.

- **"The TOP" Function - Variant 1**

Lying on her back, supported and blanketed via the thighs of the man who penetrates her in a guided press-up, the woman is massaged tightly on the hands, taking up the penis' entire length.

This challenge needs to be carried out after the "Head" role to preserve the lovers' sexual organs in touch. At the second, when the man feels close to the ejaculatory climax, he has to pause his moves and sit there for at least 30 seconds to stop ejaculation.

Similar to "the top" position, this position gives each fan intense pleasure, and it favors the accumulation of sexual strength in the genital region.

The fans want to focal point their interest in the center of the forehead to sublimate the sexual electricity at the sixth chakra level (AJNA CHAKRA).

Therefore the fans extend their control energy over the sexual energy.

- **"Driving the Nail Home" Role - Variant 1**

The man plunges into her with deep thrusts, going through her, lying on top of her, aiding himself on his soles.

She receives him with tightly spread thighs proper up to the hilt. The man may additionally both cross his pelvis lower back and forth or up and down.

Contrary to all assumptions in this function, the female does not have to be passive. She's bought to grasp the man's thighs with her fingers and pull him in opposition to her to attain deeper into her vagina.

When the man feels shut to the ejaculatory orgasm, he ought to pause his movements for a few seconds and focus his interest on the crown to direct the sexual energy through the spine to the crown. Same even for the woman.

- **"Driving the Nail Home" Role - Variant 2**

To both lovers, face-to-face roles are enjoyable. They motivate them to seem at every other, to see how their desire mounts and, above all, to share caresses among themselves.

The female lies behind her. Facing her, leaning on top of her, the guy plunges with full thrusts of his loins into the woman's vagina. He then places her fingers on his back.

The man's erected penis fills up the woman's vagina. The man plunges into her profoundly and firmly with his pelvis, touching her pelvic intimately so that she can sense his member's presence all the better.

In this place, the female is not passive. Holding the man's thighs, she pulls the man's pelvis toward her to reach deeper in his thrusts. The robust thrusts of the man in this position might also provoke the awakening of the Kundalini of the woman. Lovers must discover their effective rhythm, which generates their Kundalini power's awakening.

This position in the artwork of sexual continence is no longer encouraged for novices, given that it encourages the attention of sexual energy in the genital region. Once the man feels shut to the ejaculatory orgasm, he needs to give up his motions and focus his attention in the crown to direct the sexual energy alongside the spine to the crown. It, too, is open to women.

- **"The TOP" Role - Variant 2**

Lying on her back, supported and protected via the thighs of the man who penetrates her in a guided press-up, the woman is firmly massaged on the hands, taking up the whole length of the penis.

He reasons his weight to fall on her even further, at the second, when he needs to feel further pleasure. The lady can experience him even more strongly at the equal time.

The "row" role offers both lovers huge pleasure and amplifies the sexual energy. This is why newbies in the art of sexual continence lovemaking need to not proceed the intercourse with it.

Both lovers have to middle their energies in the discipline of the heart to sublimate the sexual electricity into greater refined sorts of energy.

When the girl senses that her lover is getting close to the climax, she has to cease the man's actions and press firmly in the center of the brow with her thumb. His interest will, as a consequence, be removed from the genital region to the forehead area, supporting the sexual strength rise along the spine.

- **"Face to Face" Function - Variant 1**

The girl lies on the back, shut to the aspect of the bed. She stretches her legs and puts one on the board. Facing her, mendacity on top of her, and the guy plunges with strong thrusts into the woman's vagina. Two of his legs unfold on the concrete, and the different one is folded.

The girl experiences his lover proper up to the hilt with thighs broadly spread. The man can explore her to the core of his heart-gently with the complete size of his penis, or-which will expand his appetite for more-he can violently insert and withdraw his penis.

This role favors the whole intimacy of the lovers' genital zones. Within the artwork of sexual continence, it is no longer endorsed for beginners, on account that it encourages the attention of sexual energy in the genital region. That is why the man should quit his motions when he reaches the pre-orgasmic stage and listen to his interest in the cardiac plexus to direct the sexual energy.

- **"The Concealed Door" Role - Variant 1**

The girl lies on her back. Next, she hugs her knees, getting her prepared to take him up to the hilt. The man, who is mendacity on the woman, insinuates himself inside her moist vagina. She then draws her legs, permitting the man's thighs to cowl her body. The man cuddles her deeply anchored in her vulva, stroking her back, her hips and her breasts. The woman can contract her vaginal muscular tissues to intensify the wishes of her lover in addition and, with the thrusts of the man, can manipulate these contractions.

The man can penetrate the woman's anal opening even in the same place if he knows she loves anal penetrations. The female has to relax her sphincters here in a high-quality way possible. The man must have full control over his penis' penetration into the warm and constricted opening, which she gives him with love and trust.

The man can chunk the woman's neck in this position, and can also tenderly caress her breasts while thrusting even deeper.

This position is enough to bring up the sexual energy and sublimate it in pure love. To obtain this extended emotion-pure love, the fanatics do not have to concentrate on the genital pleasure in the course of this position. Still, they have to concentrate their interest on the region of the coronary heart and grow to be aware of the flying feeling this role produces. If the fanatics go away them to the flying sensation, they like they're lost in an ocean of pure love.

3.5 Sitting Positions

- **"The Pivot" Role**

During intercourse, the female turns as a horizontal wheel around a vertical axis right around the man. The man pinches her and caresses her nipples taking advantage of these places. For her part, she may fondle the reclining man's breast, whose penis makes use of her in flesh and blood like a pivot. She takes up solely the length of her penis through squirming and elevating herself a bit, and she needs to look in herself. The "pivot" position approves both guys and girls to get a strong focus of mind. This is why human beings who have commenced to exercise sexual continence are recommended for this role.

- **"Seesawing" Function**

Sitting slightly earlier than the thighs of the man, she takes the section of his penis solely, so that either of them can manipulate the length inserted in turn. Kneeling she can stroke the man's legs; aiding herself on his hands and making quick thrusts with his pelvis he comes to meet her halfway or acts as if he have been going to withdraw completely, leaving her almost absolutely to penetrate her open vagina again, which in this role is very moist. This gives her an attractive rubdown upwards.

- **"The Closed and the Opened Ring" Function**

Here we have two absolute submission positions, the place the lady only receives the man to the extent he wants. He penetrates her in accordance with his pattern, entertaining himself with the softly and frequently aggressively inserting and removing his penis.

The lovemaking girl will use this role to swing softly with her own thighs on the thighs of her lover and supply her vagina, which is bombarded from below.

Such two variations of the function of "the closed and the open ring" enable the man to turn out to be extra aware of the strength of pleasure and additionally to decrease it by stopping the actions when he feels that he is reaching the climax. Both fanatics have to core their attention in the middle of the brow for the sublimation of sexual energy. It will trigger a clear-minded nation in each lover, which will help them modify and sublimate the sexual strength in higher energies.

- **"Pincers from the Front" Position**

Here is every other so-called resting place for the man, whose manly member is skillfully massaged from the front by way of the woman.

Man is no longer going. The girl pushes into her vagina the complete size of the penis, supporting herself on her hands and squeezing her member like a pair of pincers. She can make motions either coming or going or repetitive motions.

The man may also both make brief thrusts with his pelvis to reach her halfway or behave as if he has been going to withdraw fully, leaving her almost entirely to enter her open vagina anew, which in this function is very humid. It gives her a horny rubdown upwards.

To novices in the art of sexual continence, this role is encouraged due to the fact it favors growing sexual energy alongside the backbone to the crown.

- **"Pincers from the Front" Role - Variant 1**

The lady lies down on her return while the man honestly fills her open vulva. Her locations her hands on his back and holds the man's hands to assist him in raising her. The girl imprisons the man's penis in this way, giving him deep pleasure. He plunges deeply and aggressively into her, so she can feel his member's size for all it's worth. The man will make gestures returned and forth, and the female desires to be tuned to her lover.

The man can gain an accurate simulation of the woman's G-spot in this position, and subsequently, she can hit the G-spot orgasm.

This function is encouraged in the art of sexual continence for the beginners due to the fact it favors growing the sexual strength alongside the backbone till the crown.

- **"The Seesaw" Function - Variant 2**

The man sits on a chair, comfortably. The lady is the one who deliberately impales upon the erect phallus of the man. This position approves fans to seem to be at each other, see how their wish rises, and, above all, to share caresses among themselves.

The man pulls her pelvis toward him via catching the woman's buttocks and fills the woman's open vulva fully. When the man feels close to the pre-orgasmic stage, he ought to cease and pay attention to his attention on the crown to direct the sexual power upwards.

The trunks of the lovers' vertical position supply them extra manipulate over the sexual energy.

To get away the man's ejaculatory orgasm and the explosive orgasm of the woman, each enthusiast needs to direct the sexual power along the spine towards the crown. Through deep happiness, this will produce a sublimation of the indispensable force.

3.6 Acrobatic Positions

- **"Buttering" Position**

The guy, securely planted in the rear position, turns around so that he can keep his physique on the hands and on the tip of the toes. The man will make both come-and-go motions in this function and circular ones.

The girl does not continue to be passive; however, she will respond with smooth pelvis movements in accordance with those produced by means of the man. In the "buttering" position, the man offers the lady with a terrific massage of her G-spot so that few ladies can withstand such stimulation without getting a deep orgasm (of course, we're speaking about non-ejaculatory orgasms).

If the man feels close to the orgasm, he ought to stop moving and concentrate his focus in the coronary heart region to sublimate the sexual force.

- **"Penetration with Deep Backward Movement" - Variant 2**

The lovers are positioning themselves in such a way that his penis is guided from the rear to her buttocks. As he pushes his penis into the vulva of the woman, he lowers her pelvis to the stage of his personal waist, whilst at the same time causing her to tip the higher section of her body upward. She helps herself on her lover's ankles to acquire an applicable equilibrium so that he can express her full vigor. The way the penis massages the vagina and the vulva sucks the penis gives the pair a deep experience of craving in this position.

Place "Penetration with deep backward movement" lets each lover raise the sexual anxiety along the spine to the top ear. The man's standing up stance makes him capable of getting greater power over sexual resources. The place of the girl determines the drift of her sexual electricity to the top of the head, and this is why she can trip more than one form of increased orgasm. This position allows the man to have adequate electricity in his arms to continue as long as feasible the function of the woman.

- **"The Seesaw" Position**

The fanatics face every other. The man then raises the lady up to her waist level. She may additionally lift him either by using his palms or around his back. Penetrated via the entire penis length, she allows her narrow vagina to slide along the erect shaft. The man can press her to himself very close, simply include that she can simplify for him with the aid of squeezing her legs tightly around his waist.

In that position, the complete vagina is massaged by using the penis. Helped by using the electricity of her body, the female will make powerful moves coming and going in sync with her lover's. Both men and women can trip profound pleasure in this way.

The man's standing fame offers him more power over sexual energy.

To quit the man's ejaculatory orgasm and the woman's discharging orgasm, each lover has to direct the sexual energy along the backbone toward the crown. This will deliver about the sublimation of the imperative strength of pleasure and pure love.

- **"The Ripe Mango Plum" Position**

With his penis, which is really thrilling for both lovers, the man plunges into her with excellent sensitivity to begin swirling motions even extra aggressively.

He sits over his lover to penetrate even more profoundly, opens her legs, and inserts his penis into the swollen mango pruning nicely furnished with blood via the adroit massage.

To each lover, this romantic function is a very thrilling one.

The woman's elevated pelvis role helps the sexual electricity to "flow" into the vicinity of the thyroid gland. This can purpose a rather accelerated form of orgasm in women.

The man has to pause his actions when he thinks that he or she is getting shut to the climax to stop his or her ejaculatory orgasm or discharge.

"The ripe mango plum" role approves the sublimation of the pure and ingenious sexual energy.

- **A variant of the "Buttering" Position**

Firmly planted in the opening of the vagina, the man leans to one side. He leans on both left and left palm or proper knee and right palm. The function of the man gives him the capability to make each come and go motions and round ones. The girl does now not continue to be passive but will reply with gentle pelvis movements, according to the men. In this role, the man presents the female with a super rubdown of her G-spot so that few ladies can withstand such stimulation without getting a deep orgasm (of course, we speak to me about orgasms besides dropping sexual energy).

The man should insert his member and dispose of as he sees fit, softly rubbing her thighs and buttocks.

If the man feels close to the ejaculatory orgasm, he ought to end shifting and focus his attention in the area of the coronary heart to sublimate the sexual energy. This can be carried out for the girl too.

- **A variant of the "Seesaw" Position**

As a long way as execution goes, this is a very complex location but very sturdy for feelings. The companions are contrary to every other. The man uplifts the girl to his waist level. She can maintain him either by his fingers or round his neck. Only at the degree of her lover's waist with her hands, the lady lets down the higher part of her body until her head hits the pillow. Then she lets down one of her thighs, and she introduces it among her legs with the help of man. The profitable exercise of this function is by tender women.

Penetrated by way of the whole penis circumference, she helps her slender vagina to slip down the shaft of the erect one. The man will press her towards himself very closely. During this place, the total vagina is massaged by using the penis. Helped through the electricity of his muscles, the man would be in a position to make solid motions coming and going.

The man's standing status offers him greater control over his sexual energy.

To escape the man's ejaculatory orgasm and the explosive orgasm of the woman, each lover ought to direct the sexual strength alongside the backbone towards the crown. In deep happiness, this will produce a sublimation of the crucial energy.

- **"Riding the Horse" Position**

The man is sustaining himself on arms and soles. The lady first rides on her husband, pushing his erect penis deep into her womb. She turns to the right after this and places her right leg below her lover's left leg and draws down her body, leaning either on one palm or on both palms. Then her locations the other leg on the man's arm, with the heel.

In this role, the lady is active, making moves to come and go. The man responds to the movements of the female by way of shifting his pelvis to penetrate his lover's entire vagina.

"Riding the horse," function offers both lovers vast pleasure and amplifies the lovemaking passion.

Both enthusiasts have to score their interest on the navel to sublimate the subtle-fire sexual energy. The enthusiasts would be full of electricity and passion.

- **"The Stallion and the Gazelle" Position - Variant 1**

The enthusiasts are contrary to each other. The man kneels beforehand of the girl and raises her up to his waist level. She positions her legs on the shoulders of the guy, imprisoning the penis of her partner, which shortly slips into her well-lubricated vagina. The man keeps the female by the hips, so each time he enters, he can penetrate as deeply as he can.

This position gives the lady a remarkable gain of inducing severe vaginal sensations.

The glans and the penis shaft arouse the top vicinity of the vagina a lot. The female has to pinch her thighs to accentuate the rubdown even further.

This position makes the female have greater manipulate over pleasure as the sexual energy flows into the brain, developing an improved orgasm form.

The man's vertical trunk role gives him a higher manipulate over the electricity of the pleasure. Therefore he will give up the ejaculation successfully.

Chapter 4: Some Most Romantic Sex Positions

Whether you are experienced or a starter, it would not matter, this chapter will provide you a range of new positions to try, and you may also already be trying some of them, but it includes tips to make them even more fun. It contains positions each for novices and experts. Feel free to attempt them the next time you jump into bed with your partner.

4.1 Sex Positions for Beginners

- **Face-To-Face**

How to Do it

Lie on your sides, and going through each other, push up on the mattress barely higher, so the hips are above your partner's. Wrap around them your pinnacle leg, and lead them inside. If it is an uncomfortable match, Lube will assist it.

Why It's Perfect For Beginners

If you are young, you'll be in touch with your associate to make sure that both of you experience comfortable. This is a satisfying place where you can relaxation — thoroughly invaded.

- **Missionary**

How to Do It

Make your accomplice shift their hips higher up the mattress while you tie your legs around them if you initiate in a missionary. This will supply you with a lot of pleasure than the missionary.

Why it's correct for starters

Missionary is an ideal beginner go-to, but this variant is a more advantageous orgasm stance. Plus, both of you are in a comfortable position just to mirror each difference and making sure that you each get what you need.

- **On Top (Modified)**

How to Do It

Push your associate in opposition to the wall or a sofa while straddling them down. They can bend their knees for even extra closeness, so they're assisting in propping you up.

Why it's desirable for Starters

This is an exquisite role on top; however, some ladies experience quite exposed or uneasy — in particular, when they're unfamiliar. This allows you to be in strength however, with a choice that is extra sexual and connected.

- **Doggy**

How to Do It

Rest on your knees and hands, and spread your legs to enable your companion to kneel behind you. Depending on your variability in height, you may additionally want your legs besides aside or nearer together.

Why it's super for Newbies

Even although you are young, you can also choose to get extra intensity. This position helps you to engage with deeper penetration and allows a clit play.

4.2 Sex Positions for Experts

- ## The Crab Walk

How to use it

If you have ever taken a gymnasium class as a child, then this position's name will simply provide some perception into how you will conclude this one. Practically, you and your associate are each attempting to get into a pseudo-crab role. He was supposed to take a seat on the floor with his legs bent, his feet flat on the ground, and his hands in assist behind him. You lower yourself onto his penis in the same function and face him, and start your bumping and grinding.

Why it seems to work

This role is just outstanding for specialists looking for things to spice up. The positioning helps you to display how deep it can get, and the perspective provides room to introduce a vibrator to the combine as well.

- ## The Bridge

How to use it

We have a function again that reminds us of something important. Yoga, anyone? You choose to lay on your again with this one while your companion gets to face you on his knees in between your thighs. From here, as you lift your hips up to touch his hips, you desire to arch your lower back when he enters you. Depending on your height, you might also find out that your feet won't be flat on the floor; however, it is not like you put too plenty of load on your back or toes as he helps your hips. When he holds firmly and thrusts in and out, your hips provide help to him.

Why Does It Work

During this position, the altitude at which his penis is in creates a deep penetration, stimulating your G-spot like whoa. It's usually in this position that either with one of his hands, he can stimulate your clitoris or do it yourself, both with hand or with a tool. Attaining an orgasm by way of actively stimulating both the G-spot and clit is, in reality, any other world.

- **Sideways Straddle**

How to use it

It's distinctly difficult to get into. It's probable recommended that you behavior a preliminary round with your clothing on, and you realize what you are walking into. But let me purpose to make this one as effortless as I can.

Initially, you want him to lay on his back, on the concrete, with both knees bent and both feet down. You're going to crawl on the pinnacle of him at that moment, dealing with off, with one of his legs caressed between your legs while you are lowering yourself onto his penis. You prefer to think about his physique is a clock, and his head is at the twelve spots: "If you straddle his right leg, your physique will factor at about 7:30. You will be switched to 4:30 if you are on his left leg. From there, you will if truth be told rock lower back and forth, rubbing towards his top thigh and pubic area. "It without a doubt sounds more complicated than it is, however it's at a degree of expertise, so if you pull it off, you get to pat yourself on the back.

Why it appears to work

This place is just about grinding and managing all the grinding, and you can decide whether and when you are going to peak.

- **The Cross**

How to use it

I adore this position; however, to be fair, getting around the first time is a little awkward. But it's just about taking matters step by way of step, same to the Sideways Straddle.

Let your man lie on his side, facing you first. Next, you favor lying perpendicular to him on your back due to the fact we are going to make a cross right here, as the title suggests. (And no, you do not have to be spiritual to do this.) From here, you desire to take your legs over his hip as you push your vagina in opposition to his pelvic place and open your legs a little so that he can get in. It might also seem like you're sitting on his lap, however, if that makes any sense, you're lying down.

Why it appears to work

Besides getting you a gold megastar in the class of experts, this one works because his constrained "range of motion" makes him remain longer, and the perspective gives first-rate clitoral stimulation. It is perfect for those guys who are going too quickly from zero to 60.

Conclusion

Hopefully, this book has helped you higher understand the relationship between guys and women and exceptional sex positions.

It is a work that to be discovered by all, each old and young; the former may additionally discover its real facts, gathered through experience, and already checked with the experience of themselves, while the latter may achieve the excellent benefits from learning expertise that others would by no means be aware of at all otherwise, or that they will find out solely when it is too late to earnings from the learning.

This book does no longer simply relies on the thought of man and his lady turning into one on the skin-to-skin, however, additionally on a non-secular level. Sex is no longer simply a physical phenomenon, as many humans would think; it is a phenomenon that consists of the body, the thoughts, the emotions, that means of these in love with one another. It is a sensual recreation in which the girl turns out to be a goddess, a favorite and preferred one. The man, in effect, is fulfilled no longer solely by himself but also by his liked wife, having executed an orgasm.

This book is a piece of recommendation with the useful resource of which sex can turn out to have a sacramental meaning, which includes our emotions and grasp that searching for to get the most enjoyment.

Here, I desire to add that the biggest sex-related false impression is an understanding that the more significant intercourse positions you know, the higher you're a lover. This is no longer necessarily real. According to female and different professionals, the sole component that matters is the emotions all companions sense when having sex, no count how many positions one would possibly be aware of. Yet capability and gaining knowledge of how to use intercourse positions also play an enormous part.

www.ingramcontent.com/pod-product-compliance
Lightning Source LLC
Chambersburg PA
CBHW061355250726
48657CB00004B/1496